Computer Monographs

GENERAL EDITOR: Stanley Gill, M.A., Ph.D.

ASSOCIATE EDITOR: J. J. Florentin, Ph.D., Birkbeck College, London

Time-Sharing Computer Systems

Time-Sharing Computer Systems

M. V. Wilkes, F. R. S.

*Professor of Computer Technology and
Head of the Computer Laboratory,
University of Cambridge*

Third Edition

Macdonald and Jane's - London and
American Elsevier Inc. - New York

© M. V. Wilkes 1968, 1972, 1975
First published 1968
Second impression 1969
Third impression 1970
Second edition 1972
Third edition 1975

Sole distributors for the United States and Dependencies and Canada:
American Elsevier Publishing Co. Inc.,
52 Vanderbilt Avenue, New York, N.Y. 10017

Sole distributors for the Continent of Europe excluding
the British Isles and Commonwealth and the Republic of Ireland:
Elsevier Publishing Company, P.O. Box 211, Jan Van
Galenstraat 335, Amsterdam, The Netherlands

Sole distributors for all remaining areas:
Macdonald and Jane's, Macdonald & Co. (Publishers) Ltd.,
Paulton House, 8 Shepherdess Walk, London, N.1.

Macdonald ISBN 0 356 08174 5
Elsevier ISBN 0 444 19525 4
Library of Congress Catalog Card No. 74–16911

Made and Printed in Great Britain by
Balding+Mansell Ltd, London and Wisbech

Contents

Preface to Third Edition

For the third edition some new material has been added and the old material has been rearranged and up-dated where necessary.

I am indebted to Professor P. Brinch Hanson and the Association for Computing Machinery for permission to reproduce as figure 3.1. a diagram that originally appeared in the *Communications of the ACM*. I am also grateful to Mr P. Hammersley, Honorary Editor of the *Computer Journal* for permission to reproduce as figure 5.2 a diagram that originally appeared in that journal.

November 1974   M.V.W.

Preface to Second Edition

This edition contains new chapters on process management and on scheduling. The latter includes an evaluation of techniques for paging, a subject about which much has been learned since the book was originally written. The material in the other chapters has been revised to take account of recent advances and in particular the section in the last chapter on the management of a computing centre offering time-sharing facilities has been re-written.

Fig. 6.1 first appeared in AFIPS Conference Proceedings Vol. 34, and I am grateful to the AFIPS Press for permission to reproduce it.

I continue to be indebted to many friends and colleagues, particularly to those at Project MAC, M.I.T., and to those in my own Laboratory. I would like to thank Professor J. C. R. Licklider, the present Director of Project MAC for enabling me to follow the evolution of the MULTICS system through a particularly interesting stage in its development. Professor F. J. Corbató, Professor J. H. Saltzer, Mr. R. C. Daley and Professor E. I. Organick have been very generous in supplying me with information. I would also like to thank Professor P. J. Denning from whom I learned much about paging during a pleasant week spent at Princeton in May 1970. Professor D. J. Howarth was good enough to give me some information about the original Atlas supervisor and later to read and approve the paragraph that appears on pages 88 and 89.

May 1971   M.V.W.

Preface to First Edition

This book is concerned with a development that is revolutionising our idea of what a computer system should be. Time-sharing burst on the world some five years ago, not as a result of the discovery of an entirely new principle, but more by the realisation that the technical means existed to make a big advance possible. There are likely to be very few large and medium-sized computer systems in the future that do not provide in some way for remote users and for central filing, in immediately accessible form, of users' data and programs.

The design of time-sharing systems is a subject that brings hardware and software experts together. In the past, the software designer has all too often been expected to cover up hardware deficiencies, and he has usually been successful in that the customer has not been conscious of the cost. I doubt that this will be so any longer. Economical and effective time-sharing will depend on getting the hardware right, and that is why I have devoted some attention in this book to such matters as memory protection.

I am indebted to the honorary Editor of *The Computer Journal* for permission to make use of two papers on 'The design of multiple-access computer systems', published in that Journal in 1967; the second was in collaboration with Dr R. M. Needham, to whom I am also indebted. I would like to thank Professor G. Capriz for permission to make use of material from the first Fibonacci Lecture which I delivered in Pisa in 1966, and which was published by the Centro Studi Calcolatrici Elettroniche presso l'Università di Pisa under the title 'Computer Graphics'. In writing on computer graphics in this book, I have drawn heavily on the work of my colleague Mr C. A. Lang, and, through him as well as directly, on the work done at M.I.T. under Professor D. T. Ross. I also had the advantage of seeing the work being done by Professor C. Levinthal and his team, also at M.I.T.

Professor R. M. Fano, Director of Project MAC at M.I.T. invited me to take part in the Summer Study with which the Project started in 1963, and he has welcomed me back on many occasions. I would like to thank him and members of the staff of the Project for their kindness. My debt to my colleagues in my own Laboratory is an obvious one, and much of the work done by them in developing the Cambridge multiple-access system is reported on in this book, some of it for the first time. In particular, I would like to mention Professor D. W. Barron, now of Southampton University, and Dr R. M. Needham, who successively led the team working on supervisor development. Other members of the team to whom I am equally indebted are Dr D. F. Hartley, Mr A. G. Fraser, Mr B. Landy, and Mr M. J. T. Guy. Mr S. R. Bourne wrote the editor referred to on p. 9.

During the writing of the book, I received much helpful advice from the colleagues I have just mentioned, and they further put me in their debt by reading and criticising the draft. Other friends who have devoted more time than they could properly spare to a similar task, and have given me detailed comments, are Professor J. C. Licklider, Professor F. J. Corbató, Professor R. R. Fenichel, Professor J. B. Dennis, Mr C. Christensen, Mr N. E. Wiseman, Mr R. Fabry, Mr H. Whitfield, Mr J. C. Gray, and Mr C. Whitby-Strevens. Mr E. N. Mutch not only read part of the manuscript, but gave me much appreciated help in seeing the work through the press. Finally, I would like to thank my secretary, Mrs B. Sharples, for her assistance, and Mrs D. Sargent for a very careful reading of the proofs.

July 1968   M.V.W.

1 A User's View of Time-Sharing

An early computer was operated by the programmer himself. Not only did he take personal charge of the computer in order to run his program, but, in searching for errors, he made free use of facilities for operating the computer under push-button control and for observing the contents of the various registers. It was not long before it was realised that this was a very inefficient way of using a scarce and expensive facility, and that it was bad management to allow machines to stand idle while the operator was thinking what to do next. In the period that followed, much attention was given to the development of efficient operating procedures so that as soon as one program had stopped another could be loaded with a minimum of delay. Hand in hand with this development went the development of program-aided error-diagnosis systems, which provided the programmer with information about what had happened to his program, and rendered it unnecessary for him to sit at the machine investigating its behaviour instruction by instruction.

While machines were still primitive little more could be done than to insist on the use of efficient operating procedures and prevent programmers from interfering with them. By the late 1950s, however, the largest machines of the period, while not very large by modern standards, were large enough to make a further step forward possible. This was to use a program, known as a *supervisor* or *monitor*, to perform some of the functions ordinarily performed by a human operator. Jobs were loaded in batches on to magnetic tape, often with the aid of a small auxiliary computer. Each batch of jobs was put through the main computer and the results came out on another magnetic tape and were subsequently printed. It was a characteristic of batch processing, as the term was originally used, that all jobs should take the same time to go through the system. Batching was a natural device to use in computers with magnetic tape as the only auxiliary storage medium, because of the high efficiency with which magnetic tapes could be written and read serially.

The development of batch processing undoubtedly improved the

1

efficiency with which the computers themselves were used. It had, however, the unfortunate effect of keeping the user away from the computer and of diminishing, especially when programs were under development, the rate at which he could work. The running of jobs through the system in large indivisible batches made it impossible for a user to obtain the results of more than a few runs a day, even if he were close at hand and received perfect co-operation from the management.

A substantial amelioration of the situation became possible as soon as random access file memories became generally available. Jobs were loaded into the file memory just as they previously had been on to magnetic tape, but the random access feature made it possible for them to be processed in some other order than that in which they were loaded. Small jobs could be allowed to overtake large jobs and jobs with special priority could be rushed through. Modern cafeteria systems exploit these capabilities to the full. Even so, to get good service, the user must be near to the computing centre or to a remote job entry terminal, and the really intimate forms of interaction with the computer are still denied to him. He may not, for example, observe and modify the action of his program while it is actually running. The term batch processing has been retained in use, even though jobs are no longer grouped into indivisible batches.

The coming of mini-computers in the early 1960s made it possible for a new generation of programmers to experience the joys of 'hands-on' operation of a computer. The advance of technology was such that many of these were more powerful than the giant machines of the early 1950s. Current mini-computers are as great an advance again on the early ones. Valuable as mini-computers are, however they do not meet all requirements, since they are limited in capacity and cannot provide the advanced software and filing facilities that are available on large systems.

The first large time-sharing system to be put into service was the Compatible Time-Sharing System (CTSS) developed at M.I.T. This development made it possible for users to be connected by a pair of wires to a powerful computer system that might be in the next room, or might be many miles away. All users, wherever they were, had instant access to the computer and could expect a response to their demands that was limited only by the fact that the computer was sharing its time between all users. The CTSS was brought into regular use in the summer of 1963, having been demonstrated earlier in various stages of development. (Corbató *et al.*, 1963.) Two separate systems were in use at M.I.T. for some years, and the longer to survive was finally closed down in July 1973. The computer on which the CTSS ran—an IBM 7090—had to be specially modified, and the fact that manufacturers of large computers have been slow to provide the hardware features necessary for efficiency has undoubtedly been a brake on the general introduction of time-sharing.

In writing this book I have drawn largely on experience first with the CTSS and later with the Cambridge Multiple Access System, developed at Cambridge University. This system was implemented on an Atlas 2 Computer and was running experimentally by March 1967. It became fully operational in 1968 and was finally closed down in 1973. (Wilkes, 1973.) A version of the system still runs at the CAD Centre of the Department of Industry.

Time-sharing facilities

The larger and more ambitious time-sharing systems set out to give the user as unrestricted access as possible to the computer. A wide range of programming languages is provided for him to use, and he can, in addition, if he feels strong enough, program in machine language. He is provided with a filing system inside the computer in which he may keep programs, data, lists of names and addresses, and anything else he pleases, in very much the way that he can keep files in a filing cabinet. He may create new files and delete old ones when he no longer needs them or when it is necessary to make room for new ones. He is provided with powerful editing facilities so that he can make changes in a file without having to re-type the whole of it. In addition to providing a service to people working at consoles, a large time-sharing system will also run jobs submitted on punched cards or punched paper tape in the ordinary way. These form what is known as the *background* in contra-distinction to the console jobs which form the *foreground*. Alternative terms that will be used are *off-line* and *on-line*. Facilities are provided for initiating a background job from a console. In addition to making it possible for the expert programmer to use the language of his choice, subsystems of various kinds can be provided for general use. For example, the JOSS-like

3

system described below ran as a subsystem on the Cambridge Multiple Access System.

A user beginning a session at a console must first attract the attention of the system. He does this by striking the key for carriage return or whatever other key may be required by the particular system that he is using. The exact interchange that follows depends on the system, but generally the user must type his name or identifier together with his problem number or account number. On the larger systems he is also required to type a password. While he does this the printing mechanism of the console is disconnected to avoid exposing the password. If the system recognises the user's particulars and if he has typed his password correctly, he is logged in and the date and time are printed. There is usually also a message of the day, a feature designed to keep users in touch with new facilities introduced and with other changes in the system. Once logged in the user communicates with the system by typing a series of commands; the individual characters of a command pass as they are typed into a buffer inside the computer and the command takes effect when the carriage return key is pressed. The exact nature of the commands varies from system to system, but all systems must provide for input and editing of information, for creating and destroying files, for examining the directory of currently existing files, for telling the user how much time he has left in his allocation, and of course, for running programs.

The means provided for creating and editing files vary from system to system and have undergone some development since the CTSS was originally demonstrated at M.I.T. In the original form of the CTSS, if the user wished to type some information—which might have been a program, a list of names and addresses, or anything else—he gave an INPUT command. This activated a program that automatically allocated serial numbers to the lines of information as they were typed. The serial numbers went up in tens in order to facilitate the insertion later of additional lines, should this become necessary. The user had the option of typing his own line numbers instead of having them allocated and typed for him by the machine. Lines numbered by the programmer were eventually sorted in order with these numbered by the machine, and, if more than one line had the same number, the last to be typed took precedence. In this way, corrections and additions could be made to the document being typed.

When all the information had been typed, the user typed the word FILE. This caused the information he had just typed to be converted into a permanent file (permanent, that is, as long as he chose to retain it) and put away into auxiliary storage. The word FILE was followed by the name that the user wished to give to the file and which would be used in all later references to it. The line numbers were stored as an integral part of the file.

Changes could be made to a file by giving an EDIT command, that is, by typing the word EDIT, followed by the name of the file that was to be edited. This command essentially put the machine back into the input mode, and the user was in the same situation as he would have been if he had just typed in the information. Additions and changes could be made by using line numbers exactly as described above for the INPUT command; when editing was complete, the amended file could be put away by typing the world FILE as before. The user could either give the amended file a new name, or retain the old one; in the latter case, the earlier version of the file was deleted.

Editors based on line numbers stored with the text are still used on some systems, but most people now prefer to use a context editor. In such an editor one has a notional pointer which starts at the top of the file and which can be stepped down. It can either be made to move over a specified number of lines, or it can be made to advance to the next line beginning with or containing some particular group of symbols. Once the pointer is on a particular line, that line can be modified or deleted, or additional lines inserted after it. Examples of editing requests that may be made are as follows:

NEXT n	move pointer down n lines
DELETE n	delete n lines
LOCATE <string>	move pointer down to the first line which contains the given character string
FIND <string>	move pointer to first line starting with the given character string
CHANGE ø <str1> ø <str 2>	replace first occurrence of character string 1 in the line being pointed at by character string 2

5

INSERT <newline>   insert the new line after the line being pointed at and move the pointer down

When each request has been complied with, the editor responds by printing the current line. Note that in the CHANGE request the symbol ø stands for any symbol that does not occur in either string 1 or string 2.

Context editors are, perhaps, not quite so sure in operation as line number editors, since every now and then the user will make a mistake in specifying the context; this, however, does not matter in the least when one is working on-line, since one is immediately made aware of the error and can put it right. Apart from having the advantage (not a negligible one) that space in the filing system is not taken up in storing line numbers, context editors are more powerful. Not only can one locate a particular line, but one can move to a context within that line. Moreover, it is possible to have global requests which cause the file to be scanned and some specified action taken whenever a certain context is encountered; for example, a given identifier can be replaced wherever it occurs by another identifier.

When a context editor is used the operations of creating a file and editing are quite distinct. Facilities are usually provided for cancelling the last character typed or for cancelling the whole of the line actually being typed, but if the user notices an error in an earlier line he must let it go and later perform a separate editing operation on the resulting file. This he does by giving the command EDIT or some equivalent. The system acknowledges this command and the user is then free to make editing requests of the type illustrated above. Some context editors allow a user, if he wishes, to refer to a line by its serial number and always print the number when printing the line. A useful facility is to be able to shift the notional beginning of a line in order to facilitate making changes in the latter part. Again it is useful to be able to repeat an editing request without typing it out again in full.

It is important to note that, in the CTSS and systems like it, an editor works on a *copy* of the file being edited. When the editing operation is complete there exist two versions of the file, the original version in the filing system and the new version held in temporary storage belonging to the editor. The user may file the edited version

6

under a new name, in which case he will have copies of both versions in the filing system for possible future use. On the other hand, he may file the new version under the same name as the old one, in which case the original version will be implicitly deleted, Similarly if a newly typed document is filed under an old name the old file will be deleted. The user must take care that he does not in this way delete valuable information. Some systems automatically keep old versions of files with a version number attached, but this facility makes great demands on disc space and has not generally been found worth while. A good filing system will provide other features that the user may exploit in order to protect information against accidental deletion (see p. 141).

The commands so far mentioned are wholly context free; that is, they are quite independent of any particular programming system or programming language. There will be other commands which enable programs written in particular programming languages (a variety may be available on a particular system) to be compiled and subsequently run. The program must first be put into the machine and filed away under a suitably chosen name. Up to this point the program is treated as an ordinary piece of text. Subsequently an appropriate command will cause the program to be compiled. When this has been done, the compiled program may either be stored in a file for future activation or it may be immediately activated. As a by-product of the compiling operation a file may be created containing the symbol table giving the memory addresses corresponding to the variables used in the program.

During the running of the program any output generated will appear on the user's console; similarly, if a statement demanding input from the console is encountered, execution of the program will be suspended until the user types the required information. A particular user's program does not remain continuously in core during the time that he is working with it; it is, in fact, continually being swapped for one or other of the many programs that are in a similar state of use and which when they are not in core reside on a drum. This swapping takes place entirely without the user being aware of what is happening, except that the machine may appear slower to him than it would if he had it entirely to himself. If a user's program halts or comes to a sticky end, it remains on the drum and the user may, if he wishes, examine it or patch it. More likely,

7

however, he will wish to modify his program in its original source language form and re-compile it.

Foreground and background

The ordinary user of a time-sharing system would like to regard on-line and off-line working as complimenting one another. He would like to be able to run one of his programs in the foreground or in the background as suited his convenience at the time. Unfortunately not all the systems currently in operation provide the necessary close integration between foreground and background. In the Cambridge system it was possible to make use of the filing system in an off-line job submitted in the usual way and it was possible to initiate such a job from a console. In the latter case the user typed a job description and put it in a file. He then gave a RUNJOB command which caused the file to be placed on the job queue. If the program had been so written that the results came out on the line printer or plotter, the the user would collect them in the ordinary way. He could, however write his program so that the results were filed, in which case, when he next returned to his console, he would examine his files to see whether the results were there. It was a management decision whether the supervisor placed a job created by the RUNJOB command at the top or bottom of the queue of off-line jobs or gave it an intermediate priority.

Systems with restricted interaction

Some systems do not allow a user to interact conversationally with a program that he has written himself but do, nevertheless, provide powerful conversational features by way of system-provided facilities. Of the latter, the most important are those that provide for the creation and editing of files. From the point of view of the user, such a system appears exactly the same as a fully interactive system except that he is not allowed to write a program with statements in it that call for input from the keyboard, nor will he ordinarily receive output from his program while it is running. Once he has activated a program he must wait for it to run to completion before he receives

8

his results. Ideally these should appear automatically on his console as soon as they are available. This was the normal mode of working on the Cambridge Multiple Access System. An alternative, not quite so convenient but acceptable, is for the results to go into a file or to be otherwise held in the system until called for. The WYLBUR system (Fajman and Borgelt, 1973) developed at Stanford University in 1967 worked in this way.

Naturally, in a system of the type just described much depends on the priority given to jobs created at consoles. If such jobs take precedence over batch jobs and if administrative overheads involved in their running are small—as for example can be achieved by using a batch monitor—a very good response can be obtained. For low priority jobs, facilities are often provided whereby the user may cause his job to be run exactly as if it had been submitted as an off-line job. In such a case results will either go to a file or be printed on a line-printer in the ordinary way.

Experience has shown that the above mode of working in which results appear automatically on the console leaves little to be desired for a wide range of work. This includes the greater part of program development in which a program is run repeatedly during the process of removing bugs. The usual and powerful tracing techniques can be used since these involve communication only in the direction of program to user. It is possible to provide an interactive system program to enable a post mortem examination of a defunct program to be made. Indeed, for the programmer who does not have the need to include console input statements in his program there is no difference between such a system and a fully interactive one.

There are two advantages in providing all the fully interactive facilities that are required by means of systems programs. One is that user programs being non-interactive may be swapped very much less frequently than they would be in a fully interactive system and the swapping overheads thereby reduced. The second is that effort can be devoted to making the interactive programs provided as part of the system short, so that they do not consume large amounts of system resources either when they are resident in core or when they are being swapped.

The designer of an operating system that provides fully interactive facilities will naturally endeavour to ensure that non-interactive programs will not incur greater overheads than they would in a system which does not provide interactive facilities for user programs. Developments that have taken place, both on the hardware and the software fronts, have made it possible for him to do this more readily, and it is no longer so necessary to stress the high cost of interactive working.

Although many users will not avail themselves of interactive facilities even if they are provided, users working in some subject areas will find them almost essential. These include artificial intelligence, computer-aided instruction, and some aspects of information retrieval. The control of experiments also affords a number of examples where interactive working is necessary. In some of these applications the 'user' is, in fact, a piece of apparatus which is being controlled on-line. In other cases the system accepts information from the experiment, processes it fully or partially, and provides the experimenter with information on which he can take further action.

Systems with restricted facilities

In addition to systems which aim at offering the user the full facilities of a large computer there are many systems that offer restricted facilities. Typically only one programming language is offered and the size of the problem that can be tackled is somewhat limited. If the facilities are well matched to the users' requirements, then restricted systems have a very important contribution to make. A pioneering system of this type was the JOSS system developed at the RAND Corporation. (Shaw, 1964; Baker, 1966.) This was a very clean system designed to appeal to the small user and its success showed clearly that there was a class of potential computer users not well catered for until that time. This included users who frequently needed to make simple calculations—of a statistical type, perhaps—which were tedious to do on a desk calculating machine, but hardly worth the overheads and delays associated with a batch-processing computer system.

Another early system that set out to give the user interactive facilities in a simple language (in this case called BASIC) was developed at Dartmouth College by J. Kemeny and T. E. Kurtz (Kurtz and Lochner, 1965), and demonstrated in 1964. This system later underwent major development and has since been widely used.

10

A very early conversational system and the first to be based specifically on the use of a cathode-ray tube display was the Culler-Fried system, demonstrated in August 1962. (Culler and Fried, 1963; Culler, 1966.) The cathode-ray tube was used both to display characters and for plotting. The system had a number of distinctive features, the originality of which deserves wider recognition.

JOSS, and systems designed in imitation of it, are best described by giving an example. The language is wonderfully natural in use and free from irritating conventions and irregularities. Half an hour on a console is quite enough to bring a beginner to the stage at which he can use the system.

The following is such a demonstration done on FIGARO, which ran as a sub-system on the Cambridge Multiple Access System. One had merely to type the command FIGARO to be in business. Note that, in the demonstration, lines beginning with a star are typed by the operator, and that those which are terminated with a star have been cancelled as far as input to the system is concerned. If the consoles available had had a two-colour ribbon, it would have been better to arrange for the user and the computer to type in different colours. This was done in JOSS and is an example of how the original JOSS system is often found to be in advance of its many imitators. Note that FIGARO (like JOSS) automatically paginates its output and numbers the pages.

```
*FIGARO IS A SYSTEM THAT ENABLES SMALL NUMERICAL CALCULATIONS*
*TO BE PERFORMED DIRECTLY FROM A CONSOLE*
*FIGARO SHOULD BE LOADED BY TYPING 'FIGARO' WHEN IN 'COMMAND' STATUS*
*AND IT WILL RESPOND BY TYPING A PAGE NUMBER AND AN ASTERISK AT THE*
*BEGINNING OF A LINE.  THIS ASTERISK INDICATES THAT IT IS*
*THE USERS TURN TO TYPE.  AN ASTERISK AT THE END OF A*
*LINE WILL CAUSE ANYTHING THAT HAS BEEN TYPED BY THE USER TO BE*
*IGNORED.  THIS FACILITY IS BEING USED TO PRODUCE THIS COMMENT*
*FIGARO IS ABLE TO TYPE THE RESULTS OF SIMPLE ARITHMETIC*
*CALCULATIONS AS FOLLOWS:*
*TYPE 1/2
        1/2 = .5
*OR*
*TYPE SQRT(4),LOG(6)
      SQRT(4) = 2
      LOG(6) = 1.7917595
*ONE MAY TYPE TEXT*
*TYPE 'WELCOME TO THE OPERA
WELCOME TO THE OPERA
*IT IS ALSO POSSIBLE FOR FIGARO TO TYPE NUMERICAL VALUES IN*
*A FORMAT DESCRIBED BY THE USER, AS SHOWN IN THE FOLLOWING EXAMPLE*
*FORM 1
     X = ,,,.,,      SQRT(X) = ...............
*X = 144.67
*TYPE X,SQRT(X) IN FORM 1
     X = 144.67     SQRT(X) = 1.20278843E1
*NOTICE THE FLOATING POINT FORMAT WITH DECIMAL EXPONENT*
*NOTE ALSO THAT WE HAVE USED A SIMPLE VARIABLE 'X' ABOVE*
*FORMS MAY BE USED TO OUTPUT HEADINGS*
*FORM 2
                    THIS IS A TABLE HEADING.
*TYPE FORM 2
FORM 2
                    THIS IS A TABLE HEADING.
*ONE MAY DEFINE FORMULAE*
*LET F(Z) = SIN(Z)**2
*LET G(Z) = COS(Z)**2
*TYPE F(.5),G(.5),F(.5)+G(.5)
      F(.5) = 2.2984885E-1
      G(.5) = 7.7015115E-1
 F(.5)+G(.5) = 1
*AND FORMULAE MAY BE RECURSIVE -*
*LET FAC(Z) = (Z>1,Z*FAC(Z-1); FRPT(Z)=0,1; 0)
*TYPE FAC(6)
      FAC(6) = 720
*TO START A NEW PAGE BEFORE THE PAGE IS QUITE FULL TYPE*
*PAGE
```

```
*IT IS POSSIBLE TO STORE PIECES OF PROGRAM;  THEY ARE CALLED STEPS*
*AND PARTS AND THE FOLLOWING EXAMPLES SHOW HOW THEY WORK*
*1 TYPE 2*X
*X = 5
*DO STEP 1
            2*X = 10
*2.1 X = 3
*2.2 Y = X**4 + COS(X)
*2.3 TYPE Y
*DO PART 2
            Y = 8.0010007E1
*ONE MAY HAVE LOOPS*
*3.1 X = I**2
*3.2 TYPE X
*DO PART 3 FOR I = (1;1;3)
            X = 1
            X = 4
            X = 9
*OR WE MAY SIMPLY LIST THE APPROPRIATE VALUES OF I*
*DO PART 3 FOR I = 3,7,33
            X = 9
            X = 49
            X = 1089
*OTHERWISE WE MAY USE A COMBINATION OF LOOPS AND LISTS*
*DO PART 3 FOR I = (1;1;2),6,(0;1;2)
            X = 1
            X = 4
            X = 36
            X = 0
            X = 1
            X = 4
*TO INSPECT ONE'S PROGRAM TYPE*
*TYPE PART 3
  3.1   X = I**2
  3.2   TYPE X
*OR*
*TYPE STEP 3.1
  3.1   X = I**2
*OR*
*TYPE ALL PARTS
  1     TYPE 2*X
  2.1   X = 3
  2.2   Y = X**4 + COS(X)
  2.3   TYPE Y
  3.1   X = I**2
  3.2   TYPE X
*WE MAY*
*TYPE FORMULA F(Z)
```

```
        F(Z) = SIN(Z)*SIN(Z)
*OR*
*TYPE ALL FORMULAE
        F(Z) = SIN(Z)*SIN(Z)
        G(Z) = COS(Z)*COS(Z)
      FAC(Z) = (Z>1,Z*FAC(Z-1); FRPT(Z)=0,1; 0)
*ALSO*
*TYPE ALL FORMS
FORM 1
   X = ,,,.,,      SQRT(X) = ...............
FORM 2
                      THIS IS A TABLE HEADING.
*AND*
*TYPE ALL VALUES
            I = 2
            X = 4
            Y = 8.0010007E1
*OR INDEED*
*TYPE ALL

    1      TYPE 2*X
    2.1    X = 3
    2.2    Y = X**4 + COS(X)
    2.3    TYPE Y
    3.1    X = I**2
    3.2    TYPE X

        F(Z) = SIN(Z)*SIN(Z)
        G(Z) = COS(Z)*COS(Z)
      FAC(Z) = (Z>1,Z*FAC(Z-1); FRPT(Z)=0,1; 0)

FORM 1
   X = ,,,.,,      SQRT(X) = ...............
FORM 2
                      THIS IS A TABLE HEADING.

            I = 2
            X = 4
            Y = 8.0010007E1
*WHERE ABOVE WE HAVE USED 'TYPE' WE MAY ALSO USE 'DELETE';  AS FOLLOWS*
*DELETE FORMULA F(Z)
*TYPE FORMULA F(Z)
I DO NOT HAVE THIS FORMULA.
*WE MAY DELETE STEPS AND PARTS OR ALTERNATIVELY REDEFINE THEM*
*HENCE*
*3.1 TYPE 'THIS IS A NEW STEP 3.1'
*HAS REPLACED THE OLD STEP 3.1 AS WE SHALL SEE*
*TYPE STEP 3.1
```

```
   3.1   TYPE 'THIS IS A NEW STEP 3.1'
*WE SHALL NOW DEMONSTRATE SOME ERRORS*
*TTYPEE X
EH?
*WE MUST RETYPE THE LINE*
*TYPE X
            X = 4
*BUT*
*TYPE S*S
S = ???
*VARIABLE S IS UNSET AND WE MAY SET IT BY*
*S = 6
*AND CONTINUE BY*
*GO
         S*S = 36
*LET US TRY A SMALL PROGRAM TO TABULATE X AND SQRT(X)*
*DELETE ALL
*2.1 TYPE FORM 1 IF X = 1
*NOTE THE CONDITIONAL INSTRUCTION*
*WE MAY PUT AN 'IF' CLAUSE AFTER ANY INSTRUCTION TO FIGARO AND MAKE*
*USE OF THE OPERATORS = < >*
*2.2 TYPE X,SQRT(X) IN FORM 2
*2.3 LINE IF X = 11
*FORM 2
         ,    ..................
*DO PART 2 FOR X = (1;2;11)
I DO NOT HAVE THIS FORM
I AM AT STEP 2.1
*FORM 1
     X       SQRT(X)
*GO
FORM 1
     X        SQRT(X)
     1     1.00000000000
     3     1.73205080756
     5     2.23606797748
     7     2.64575131106
     9     3.00000000001

I CANNOT COMPLETE YOUR FORM
I AM AT STEP 2.2
*THIS IS BECAUSE '11' CANNOT BE TYPED IN ONE FIGURE*
*FORM 2
         ,,   .................
*WE TIDY THE LAYOUT*
*2.15 LINE IF X = 1
*2.05 LINE IF X = 1
```

```
*SINCE WE DO NOT WISH TO CONTINUE WE EXIT FROM THE ERROR STATE*
*BY TYPING*
*DONE
*DO PART 2 FOR X = (1;2;11)

FORM 1
      X        SQRT(X)

      1       1.0000000000
      3       1.7320508076
      5       2.2360679775
      7       2.6457513111
      9       3.0000000000
     11       3.3166247903

*APART FROM SIMPLE VARIABLES ONE MAY USE VECTORS*
*A(6) = 3
*TYPE A(6)
        A(6) = 3
*OR MATRICES*
*B(1,4) = 5
*TYPE B(1,4)
        B(1,4) = 5
*A SIMPLE WAY TO INPUT THE VALUES OF A VECTOR IS WITH 'DEMAND'*
*4.1 DEMAND A(I)
*DO PART 4 FOR I = (1;1;3)
        A(I) = 34
        A(I) = SIN(A(1)) + 56
        A(I) = =1.56E-2
EH?
I AM AT STEP 4.1
*AN ERROR IN THE INPUT*
*GO
        A(I) = -1.56E-2
*TYPE ALL VALUES
         I = 3
         X = 11
      A(1) = 34
      A(2) =  5.6529083E1
      A(3) = -.0156
      A(6) = 3
    B(1,4) = 5
*IN THE DEMAND LOOP FIGARO HAS TYPED EVERYTHING EXCEPT THE VALUES*
*OF THE ELEMENTS AND THESE WERE TYPED BY THE USER*
*TO ASSIST WITH PAGE LAYOUT THE PAGE AND LINE NUMBERS ARE AVAILABLE*
*TYPE PN,LN IN FORM 7
I DO NOT HAVE THIS FORM
```

16

```
*FORM 7
     PAGE NUMBER =    ,,        LINE NUMBER =      ,,
*GO
     PAGE NUMBER =    6         LINE NUMBER =      3
*THERE IS OF COURSE A VARIABLE SET TO 3.14159...*
*TYPE PI
          PI = 3.1415926
*THIS EXAMPLE SHOWS THAT MULTICHARACTER NAMES MAY BE USED.   IN FACT UP TO*
*FOUR CHARACTERS LONG*
*HERE ENDETH THE FIRST LESSON*
*QUIT
```

The FIGARO sub-system was written by D. Barton, and this demonstration was devised by R. M. Needham and D. Barton.

The use of display terminals

A time-sharing system is likely to have a large number of terminals associated with it. For this reason the cost of an individual terminal is a critical matter and it is likely that the majority of terminals will be of a simple character. Early experience showed that a teletype-writer was a surprisingly adequate terminal for many users; the low rate at which information could be typed, while not being exactly matched to users' needs, did not fall impossibly short. The desire, however, to be able to inspect files and results more quickly led to an interest in typewriter-like devices in which the mechanical printer was replaced by a cathode-ray tube on which 'soft copy' could be displayed. Connected through a telephone line to a computer, such a device was capable of displaying characters at least ten times as fast as a teleprinter could print them. The lack of permanently printed copy proved to be less of a drawback than might have been supposed, provided that it was possible to get printed output from a line printer without too much delay.

Video display units (VDUs), as they are called, are of two types. In one the beam is deflected to draw out the individual characters; these are known as steered beam VDUs. In the other the picture is formed by means of a raster as in the case of an ordinary television set. In both cases the display must be animated, that is, traced out repeatedly at high speed. For this reason sufficient storage is needed within the unit to hold a complete tubeful of information. This storage is usually of the semiconductor type, and it is to the rapid development that has taken place in semiconductor technology that we owe the self-contained inexpensive VDU. Raster-type VDUs capable of displaying a large amount of information tend to be somewhat less expensive than comparable devices working on the steered beam principle; some of the latter, however, have a line drawing capability which gives an added value where it can be exploited.

Animation can be avoided by using a cathode-ray tube of the storage type in which a display once traced out is stored electrostatically inside the tube. Storage tubes can be used to display information at high density. Selective erasure of individual characters is not possible, nor is interaction with a light pen (see p. 114). Some storage tubes, however, have a writing mode which enables information to be displayed but not stored. It is possible to provide the user with a pointer, implemented in this mode, that he can move about the screen to indicate the particular part with which he wishes to be concerned. Storage tubes can be used to display diagrams as well as alpha-numeric characters and can be fitted with attachments that produce hard copy after the style of an office copying machine.

If it is desired to exploit the full capabilities of a display and permit the user to interact directly with it by means of a light pen, a Rand tablet, or some similar device (see p. 114), then one is led to make use of a satellite digital computer for controlling the display. Discussion of satellites is left for Chapter 6.

2 Early Systems and General Principles

From the system designer's point of view, the important thing about time sharing is that we now regard the users as being within the system instead of outside. One of the peripheral devices that can be connected to a computer is now seen to be a console with a human operator working at it, and knowledge of the operator's characteristics is as important to the system designer as a knowledge of the characteristics of, say, a magnetic-tape deck. Unfortunately, these characteristics cannot be expressed with the same unambiguous precision. In the first place, a user adapts his response to the system in such a way as to take advantage of its good features and to circumvent its bad ones. In the second place, a system will only acquire users to whom it can give reasonable satisfaction; improvements to a system can bring about big changes in the composition of the user population by making the system attractive to a wider circle of users. It is not, therefore, legitimate to take measurements of the performance and response times of users on a particular system and to assume that these will apply to the users of some other system. This fact would appear to impose a severe limitation on the utility of simulations of systems still in the design stage.

We are still a long way from knowing how best to exploit, in the interests of the smooth running and throughput of the system as a whole, the human intelligence that is now available within it. In matters of scheduling and recovery from error, in particular, human beings should be able to complement the efforts of the supervisor; one of the main problems, however, is how to present them with the information on which they can act.

Interrupts

Special provision for interrupting the currently running program must be made in the design of a computer if time sharing is to be possible. The simplest method is to include in the repertoire of

20

instructions a conditional jump instruction which senses a flip-flop that can be set, or reset, from outside the computer; whether or not a jump takes place depends on the state of that flip-flop. If this instruction is included in the main loop of a program in such a position that it is encountered frequently, then a jump to an entirely different program can be brought about externally by changing the state of the flip-flop. For some purposes, this method of organising time sharing is very satisfactory. It has the advantage that interruption of a program can take place only at points that the writer of that program has himself chosen. However, it is very inconvenient to have to depend on the writer to scatter a suitable number of conditional jump instructions in each program that is liable to be interrupted; moreover, the system would not make possible the immediate interruption of the running program on the receipt of an external stimulus. Most modern computers are, therefore, provided with a system whereby an external stimulus can interrupt the running program directly.

In a typical interrupt system, such as one might expect to find in a small computer, there is a set of flip-flops which can be sensed individually by the program, or read as a word into the memory. One of these flip-flops is associated with each peripheral device in such a way that it becomes set when that device requires attention; for example, a paper-tape punch, having punched the character it has been given, will cause its associated flip-flop to become set, and so indicate that it is ready to receive another character. When a flip-flop becomes set, the hardware causes the content of the program counter to be saved in a register in core memory set aside for this purpose; it then brings about a jump to a fixed place in memory, where a routine for servicing interrupts is to be found. This routine causes the content of the accumulator, and perhaps of other arithmetic registers as well, to be saved, and proceeds to determine which peripheral caused the interrupt. Control is then sent to an appropriately written subroutine. When the interrupt has been serviced, control returns to the main interrupt routine which ascertains whether any other interrupt flip-flops have become set during the time that the first interrupt was being serviced. If so, these interrupts are serviced in the same way as before by calling on appropriate subroutines. When there are no further interrupts to be serviced, the arithmetic registers are restored to their former values, and control returned to the main program. The interrupt system may be disabled by the program; if this is done, the interrupt flip-flops may still become set, but the program is not actually interrupted until the system is re-enabled.

In the system that has just been described, certain interrupts may be given priority over others by designing the interrupt routine suitably. In more elaborate interrupt systems, to be found on larger machines, the interrupt flip-flops are often divided into groups, to which the hardware accords an order of priority. When a low-priority interrupt is in process of being serviced, it is possible for a higher-priority interrupt to receive attention; in other words, there can be interrupts within interrupts. Sufficiently comprehensive means for enabling and disabling the interrupt system must be provided to permit an interrupt routine to protect itself against further interrupts at certain critical moments when processor registers are being saved. When the servicing of an interrupt, and of any higher-priority interrupts that have occurred within it, has been completed, the hardware directs attention to any interrupts of lower priority that are waiting to be serviced.

Interrupts can also be brought about by internal, rather than external, stimuli. They are then usually known as *traps* or *faults*. Typical traps are caused by accumulator overflow, or by an attempt on the part of a program to access a section of the memory that is locked out.

Time sharing was originally introduced in order to make it possible for a computer to interact efficiently with its peripheral devices. For example, in the Electrologica X1 (Loopstra, 1959), which was one of the first commercial computers to have this facility, users' programs did not communicate directly with the paper-tape punch used for output; instead, when a character was to be put out, the user program would send control to a special output routine that was permanently resident in core. The output routine would either send the character directly to the punch or, if the punch were busy, place it, together with any other waiting characters, in a reserved part of memory known as a *buffer*. Control would then revert to the user program. As soon as the punch had reached the end of its punching cycle, it would send an interrupt signal to the computer. This would cause the immediate halting of the user program, and the sending of control to a routine that would transfer the next character in the buffer to the punch. The punch would continue in motion and, in due course, punch the character that it had been given; meanwhile, the interrupt routine would have returned control to the user program.

22

Input from the paper-tape reader was buffered in a somewhat similar way. The net result was that the arithmetic unit was not needlessly held up waiting for the operation of an input or output device.

Requests for attention from peripherals fall into two classes, namely, those that must be serviced within a certain time if information is not to be lost, and those which can wait as long as need be. An example of the first is a card reader of the type that sets a card into motion, and then interrupts the computer as each row of holes comes into position ready to be read. The reading must be performed within a short interval of time after the interrupt is received. On the other hand, an interrupt coming from a printer when the printing of a line of characters has been accomplished need not be attended to immediately since, if another line is not sent, the printer will merely come to rest and wait.

Object programs

In describing a time-sharing system, a distinction must be made between user programs and programs that perform various administrative or switching functions. The latter are more or less interconnected, and are known collectively as the supervisor. This is a natural extension of the meaning of this term which, it has already been mentioned, was originally introduced in connection with the early batch-processing systems. The term monitor may be taken as synonymous with supervisor. Instead of user program, it is often convenient to use the term *object program*; this includes programs which, while belonging to no individual user, are treated by the system in exactly the same way as user programs.

It is necessary that object programs shall not be able to interfere with the supervisor, and modern computers have memory protection systems that prevent an object program from having access to unauthorised parts of the memory. This usually implies that there must be a privileged mode of operation in which there are no restrictions on memory access, and in which the lockout limits for the non-privileged mode can be set. The supervisor itself runs in the privileged mode. Object programs are not allowed to operate input and output devices themselves, but must do so by making a call on the supervisor.

Lack of adequate memory protection in a computer can be circumvented by designing an interpretive system. One is then in effect programming for a pseudo-machine which can be endowed with all the features that the system programmer desires. It can be given a floating-point arithmetic unit if the basic computer does not have one at all, or a cleaned up version of what was originally provided. JOSS is an example of a system that was programmed interpretively. In such a system, control never leaves the supervisor and, in consequence, once the supervisor is completely debugged nothing can go amiss. It would not, however, be practicable to design in this way a system in which the user was allowed to make use of compilers or to write in machine code. Detailed discussion of memory protection is reserved until Chapter 4.

Some parts of the supervisor, especially those connected with certain aspects of scheduling and accounting, can be written exactly as though they were object programs. Others require to be specially privileged in one way or another. In the interests of easy testing and maintenance, the system designer should do his best to make it possible for those routines to be written in a manner that differs as little as possible from that in which object programs are written. They can then be developed, at any rate partially, under normal computer service conditions. There is a limit to what can be done in this respect, however, and the more intimate sections of the supervisor, especially those dealing with the operation of mechanical peripherals, can only be developed on a machine dedicated for the time being to the purpose. Since work with a dedicated computer is both slow and costly, a prime objective in the design of any large software system is to minimise the amount of dedicated computer time that will be needed to develop it.

Simple swapping

Given a comprehensive hardware interrupt system, a digital clock that can bring about interrupts, and some form of memory protection, combined with a magnetic drum of fairly large capacity, it is possible to establish an elementary form of time sharing based on simple swapping. One active object program only is in core at any time, other active programs being held on the drum. When the program currently in core has exhausted the quantum of time allowed to it, reached the end of its work, or come to a point at which it is held up for input or output, it is sent back to the drum and another program loaded.

The principles are well illustrated by an experimental system developed for a small computer at Bolt, Beranek and Newman, Inc., (BBN) in Cambridge, Mass. (McCarthy, Boilen, Fredkin, and Licklider, 1963.) This system was in operation as early as September 1962, and enabled five users to work simultaneously at five typewriters. The computer was a DEC PDP1 with 8K words* of core memory, of which 4K were occupied permanently by the supervisor and 4K were used for users' programs. There was a drum with accommodation for 22 sectors of 4K words each. A special drum interface was designed and constructed that would enable the content of user core to be dumped on to one sector of the drum at the same time that the content of another drum sector was being transferred into core.

The computer came equipped with an interrupt system very similar to that described in the last chapter. It was modified to have privileged and unprivileged modes of operation. In the unprivileged mode, any attempt by the program to operate an input or output device, to execute a stop instruction or other illegal instruction, or to attempt a reference to that part of the core memory that contained the supervisor, would set one of the interrupt flip-flops and bring about a trap. A further addition to the computer was a clock, consisting of a simple oscillator, that would bring about an interrupt on one of the other channels every 20 milliseconds.

Contained within the supervisor were a number of routines. One of these was responsible for communicating with the typewriters on a character by character basis. It was divided into sections, one for each typewriter, and associated with each section were two buffer areas of core, one for input and one for output, each capable of holding a whole line of characters. When a typewriter has completed the typing of a character an interrupt was sent to the computer, interrupts from different typewriters going to different inputs. The interrupt routine caused control to pass to the appropriate section of the typewriter routine. If the character had been typed by the user, the typewriter routine would place that character in the buffer and return

*K = 1024

control; if the typewriter had typed a character sent to it by the computer, the typewriter routine would send to the typewriter the next character to be typed, if any. The routine always knew whether it was the user or the computer that typed the last character since, in the former case, it would itself have sent the character to the typewriter. It will be seen that the typewriter routine was quite independent of other parts of the supervisor, and was merely responsible for transferring characters between the buffers and the typewriters.

The next routine in the supervisor was responsible for handling traps that occurred during the running of a user program. Such a program ran in non-privileged mode, and an attempt to obey an input or output instruction, or to perform one of the actions listed above, would lead to a trap. The trap routine sent control to a routine that examined the instruction that caused the trap. If this were of the output type, the character that the user program was attempting to put out was transferred to the output buffer, and control was sent to the appropriate section of the typewriter routine. If the instruction were of input type, a character was transferred from the input buffer to the program. User programs did not have to be written in any special way to run on this system; the supervisor, in effect, simulated exactly the normal action of the input and output instructions.

The final supervisor routine to be described was essentially a *scheduling algorithm*, although, in this system, the scheduling rules were extremely simple, being based on a circular queue or so-called round robin. The scheduling algorithm was entered every time a clock interrupt occurred and, if it were found that the program in core had exhausted its quantum of time (140 milliseconds), that program was swapped for the next program on the queue that was in the *working state*, that is, was ready to run. A program could also be swapped out because the output buffer associated with it was full, or because it had asked for a character from the input buffer and there was nothing there. An attempt by a user program to stop the computer, or execute an illegal instruction, would also cause the program to be swapped out. Programs that had been swapped out for reasons other than having exhausted their quantum of time would not be in the working state; a program swapped out because the output buffer was full would be returned to the working state when the buffer had almost emptied, and a program swapped out for want of an input

26

character would be returned to the working state as soon as that character had arrived.

The BBN system contained a routine within the supervisor which gave the user certain facilities for postmortem examination of a dead program, and for performing patching operations. These facilities will not, however, be described here.

This pioneering experiment showed what, perhaps, is in danger of being forgotten, that a simple and useful time-sharing system for a small computer need not be complicated.

The CTSS

Although the CTSS was much more elaborate and ran on a much larger computer (an IBM 7090), it resembled the BBN system in its general mode of operation. Part of the core was permanently occupied by the supervisor and the programs belonging to the users resided on a magnetic drum from which they were brought one by one into the core under the control of a scheduling algorithm. User programs did not communicate directly with mechanical peripheral devices, such as line printers and card readers. Instead, they made a call on the supervisor, which transferred the information to or from a buffer area in protected core. Transfer of information between the buffers and the peripherals took place asynchronously with the operation of the user's program. The organisation and timing of this transfer was another of the functions of the supervisor.

Much new ground was broken in the CTSS particularly in relation to the organisation of a disc-based filing system. If this and many of the other features of the CTSS are not described here, it is because so much of what has been learned from that system has passed into the general stock of knowledge and is discussed at its appropriate place elsewhere in the book.

Various modifications to the computer were necessary before the system could be implemented. In common with other computers of its generation, the IBM 7090 had no provision at all for memory protection. Moreover, there was a need to increase the amount of core memory available in order to provide accommodation for the supervisor and still allow the user the normal 32K words for his program. Accordingly, a second memory module of 32K words was fitted, together with a relocation register and two memory protection registers; numbers set in these registers operated as bounds outside which the module could not be accessed. There was a program operated switch for changing over from one memory module to the other. This switch also functioned as a mode switch; in privileged mode (called normal mode in CTSS terminology) the supervisor memory module was connected and privileged operations, such as setting memory protection registers and operating input and output devices, were allowed. User programs operated in what was called special mode with the second memory module connected. Attempted violations by the user program caused a switch to privileged mode and an entry to the trap routine. Deliberate violation by a user program was a regular way of calling on the supervisor for input and output and other purposes. Other modifications to the computer were the provision of a clock interrupt system and an IBM 7750 communication system through which the consoles were connected. The configuration included a disc file.

The mode of action of the supervisor may best be explained by describing the various states through which a program passed during the time that it was active. A session started by the user going through the logging-in sequence; when the system had accepted him and typed R, for READY, he was said to be in *command status*. The system then interpreted anything that he typed as a command and searched the command directory for the corresponding program. He was now said to be in the *waiting command* state, and was requesting attention from the scheduling algorithm. Once his program had been scheduled for execution, it was said to be in the *working* state. At any given time a number of user programs might be in the working state, but only one could, of course, actually be loaded and using the processor. When a user program attempted to read a line of input from its console, the supervisor examined the input buffer belonging to that user. If there was a line in the buffer, that line was transferred to the user's program which continued to run. If there was no complete line in the buffer the supervisor placed the user program in the *input wait* state. It was then temporarily ignored by the scheduling algorithm until the user had typed a complete line. A program might go into the *output wait* state if it generated so much output that the output buffer was in danger of overflowing. There was also a *file wait* state into which a program was put if it attempted to open for writing a file that was already open, or if it attempted to open for reading a file that another program had opened (or was waiting to open) for writing. Programs in one of the wait states were automatically returned to the working state when the condition that caused them to be held up had cleared.

When a program had finally terminated, the supervisor placed it in the *dead* state; if, however, it came to an end by reason of some violation, or if it specifically so requested, it was placed in the *dormant* state. A dormant program could be restarted by the user or subjected to post-mortem examination.

Some commands were executed by routines associated with the supervisor and kept permanently in core. Others involved the loading of a program from the disc. One program could bring about the loading of another program. The supervisor was unaware of whether it was executing a program corresponding to a system command or a program written by a user. Commands other than those executed by supervisor routines were, in fact, programs that had been written at some time or other as object programs, and had been placed by the management in the supervisor's file directory.

When a user's program became dead or dormant, the user automatically reverted to command status. In general, except when his program was dead, the user had a program that was either running in the processor or existed as a core image on the disc. Various post-mortem facilities enabled him to examine this core image, and he could, if he wished file away a copy of it for future reactivation.

At any one time there might be some 20 or 30 users logged-in. The maximum number was not fixed but could be set by the management. Only a small number of them would have jobs in the working state, and the number would fluctuate from moment to moment. The jobs would differ greatly in the core space they occupied and in the running time they needed. It was the function of the scheduling algorithm to determine which of the programs in the working state should be run next, and how much time each should be allowed.

The design of a scheduling algorithm for such a system calls for careful consideration. A round robin in which each program when loaded is offered the same quantum of time is not completely satisfactory. Corbató designed and implemented for the CTSS an algorithm in which there were a number of queues or *levels*. A program which did not terminate, or reach an input or output wait, during a period of activation was transferred to the next lowest level unless it happened to be on the lowest level already. When its level had been reduced by one, a program was accorded a lower priority by the algorithm, but given twice as much time when it came to be activated. In this way the expenditure of an excessive amount of time in swapping long-running programs was avoided. The level to which a program went when it was first activated, or when it was reactivated after a wait, was determined according to the amount of core space it occupied, larger jobs going to a lower level.

One intended consequence of the algorithm was that users whose programs ran to completion, or reached an input or output wait, on their first activation got a better response from the system than did other users. In fact, the majority of programs were of this kind; this was a consequence partly of the choice made of the parameters of the algorithm, and partly of the tendency of users to adapt their behaviour so as to get a good response. The algorithm also gave a better response to users whose programs were small, and this had a similar effect on the behaviour of users. At one point in the history of the CTSS, the program size threshold above which the algorithm discriminated against a user was reduced from 10K to 4K words. No announcement of this change was made, but it was observed that within a few weeks the mean length of users' programs had been reduced by 40 per cent.

Experience with another early large-scale time-sharing system that became operational in June 1963 at the System Development Corporation (Schwartz *et al.*, 1964) confirmed the experience with the CTSS that it is necessary to cater separately for small brief jobs and for longer ones. In that system two queues were provided, and jobs were transferred to the second queue when it appeared that they were taking a long time on the regular queue. Once on the second queue, they received larger amounts of time but at less frequent intervals. It was found desirable on this system also to give a higher priority to small programs than to large ones.

The reader will appreciate from what has just been said that the design of the scheduling algorithm can influence profoundly the behaviour of users and, by making the system attractive for some types of work rather than others, determine the use that will be made of the system. A scheduling algorithm designed to suit the needs of one community of users would not necessarily be suitable for another community.

The swapping algorithm on the CTSS was not quite as simple as the references to simple swapping may suggest. When a swap took place only enough of the contents of core were copied on to the drum to make room for the incoming program. Thus, it might happen that, when a large program was sharing the computer with a number of smaller ones, part of the large program would remain in core all the time. This could lead to a useful saving of swapping time, particularly when large background jobs were being run in conjunction with a light foreground load of small jobs. It was decided not to develop the CTSS further in the direction of sharing core between several user programs, although the hardware facilities would have made such development possible.

Console connection

An essential requirement for a modern time-sharing system is an efficient means of attaching a substantial number of consoles to the computer, and the device used for this purpose is sometimes referred to as a *multiplexer*. In the BBN system, there were only five typewriters and it was practicable to connect these to the computer through separate input channels and to provide each of them with a separate interrupt line. Now that consoles are more numerous and have often to be connected over leased or switched lines, it is usual for each console to be connected to the multiplexer by a pair of wires and for the multiplexer to communicate with the computer through a single data channel. The multiplexer converts incoming characters from serial to parallel form, and passes them, together with the number of the line along which they have come, to the computer. It similarly performs the reverse operation for outgoing characters.

It is usual to operate consoles on a *duplex* basis; that is to say, signals in the two directions are sent along channels that are logically separate, even though they may be provided by means of a single pair of wires. There is then no connection within a console between the keys and the printing mechanism, and anything typed by the user will not be printed unless it is echoed back by the computer. Not only does this provide a check on transmission errors, but it also enables printing to be dispensed with when it would be inconvenient, for example, during the typing of passwords.

The routine that acts as an interface between the multiplexer and the rest of the supervisor will be known as the *multiplexer routine*. It is probably best that the echo should, in normal circumstances, be provided by the multiplexer routine, but that this routine should be so designed that any program, whether a system program or a user program, can turn off the echo. This enables the logging-in program to turn off the echo when the user is typing his password. It also enables special echoing features to be provided when these are required. For example, the command interpreter can be designed so as to recognise a command by the first few letters typed and to supply the rest automatically, or to insert into the command as typed additional 'noise' words designed to improve readability. Commands can be provided whereby the console user himself can turn the echo from the multiplexer routine on or off. This is useful if he finds that he is getting two echoes, one from the multiplexer routine and one from some program with which he is communicating.

The multiplexer can be based on a small general purpose computer. This had the advantage of flexibility, and means that communication with the users does not break down when the main system goes out of action, so that they can be kept in touch with what is happening. The small computer can perform some of the functions that would otherwise be performed in the multiplexer routine.

For all ordinary work it is sufficient if a complete line of information is always handed over by the multiplexer routine to the supervisor or user program as the case may be. This simplifies the situation if a small interface computer is used, since that computer need interrupt the main computer only on the receipt of a carriage return. However, for some purposes, character by character interaction with the computer is required. With the above system this could only be secured by typing a carriage return after each character. This would be objected to by users since it would spoil the layout of their work; if a suitable non-printing character is available on the keyboard, then this particular objection can be met by designing the multiplexer routine so that it will recognise that character as being equivalent in every way to carriage return. Serious character by character interaction with the system would, however, hardly be possible if each character had to be followed by another symbol; if such interaction is required, a better plan is to design the multiplexer routine so that it can be set to signal the arrival of every character and not just the arrival of a carriage return.

Escape facilities

An example of a function that can conveniently be performed in the multiplexer routine is giving effect to corrections made by the user in the course of his typing. This is sometimes known as *local line editing*. The user may wish to cancel the character he has just typed or to cancel the whole line; it is not possible at this level to give him facilities for cancelling earlier lines, since these will have been passed on by the multiplexer routine to the supervisor, or to his program, as the case may be. Two characters from the character set may be allocated for local line editing, one deleting the last character in the input buffer and the other deleting the whole line. However, these characters are not then available for general use and this is likely to be inconvenient. This difficulty may be overcome, although at the cost to the user by having to type two characters instead of one, by making use of an *escape character*; this is some little used character whose function is to indicate that the next character to be typed has a special significance. @ is used for this purpose in Cambridge and if followed by the letter C indicates that the character just typed is to be cancelled; if followed by the letter L it indicates that the whole line is to be cancelled, and in this case the computer supplies carriage return and line feed symbols. If @ is followed by @ then @ is placed in the input buffer.

The advantage of providing local line editing facilities in the routine that interfaces with the multiplexer is that they are then available in a standard form at all times and for all purposes. A system designer who leaves the provision of such facilities to the writers of individual subsystems is not doing his job.

Terminal devices work in a variety of codes and an important function that must be performed by the multiplexer routine is conversion to standard internal code. It should be possible for different devices connected to the same multiplexer to have different conversion tables. It is highly desirable that the internal code should be shift free, or otherwise editing operations are made more difficult

33

than they need be. This requires that at least seven bits should be available for each character; a machine with 8-bit addressable bytes is ideal.

The reader should think of the user sitting at his console and, with the co-operation of the multiplexer routine, pushing characters into his input buffer; at the same time the program that is working for him—being a part of the supervisor or one that he has written himself—is sucking characters from it. If the user types too fast, his buffer will become full and he will receive a message to that effect, while if the program demands characters before they have been typed it will be held up. In some systems the buffer is large enough for the user to be able to type several commands or lines of information ahead of their being required; for example, he can type one command while the previous command is still being executed. This facility is known as *type ahead*. In other systems, the user can only put one line of information at a time into his buffer and the buffer is cleared on completion of each command. In such systems the user must wait for each command to be executed before he types the next one.

In all time-sharing systems there is a clearly defined command status and when the user has this status anything that he types goes directly to the supervisor which interprets it as a command. When a command is being executed his console is connected to an object program or system program as the case may be. In the latter state it is, however, necessary for the user to have some power to communicate directly with the supervisor. A minimum requirement is that he should be able to abort or suspend a program when he realises that he has made a mistake, when the program has gone into the loop, or when it is typing quantities of inofrmation that he does not need. The result of aborting or suspending a running program in this way is to restore the user to command status. This may be a more drastic action than is required; for example, if the user is operating in a subsystem it may be required to restore him to what corresponds to command status within the subsystem. Thus, while using the editor, he may wish to interrupt some action that he has called for, such as the typing of a piece of text, but still remain within the editor. These facilities can be provided by making use of the escape character already mentioned in connection with local line editing. For example, @QUIT or @Q might cause the running program to be aborted and the user returned to command status. @I might cause the program to be trapped and then act in any way its writer has prescribed. Teletypes and some other consoles have a *break key* which can be used momentarily to open-circuit the line. The multiplexer can be de-designed to recognise this event and pass a signal to the computer. The break key is often used for sending signals to running programs, but its use would not appear to have any special advantage over the use of the regular keys except in systems in which the consoles are not connected in the duplex mode.

It is possible to go further and enable the user to give more general commands to the supervisor while his program is running. For example, it might be possible for him to type USERS? (preceded by the escape character) and the supervisor would tell him how many users there were on the system and what they were doing. There does not seem to be any good reason, however, why the user who wishes to ask questions of this type should not wait until he next returns to command status. There is a stronger case for making it possible for him to enquire about the progress of a running program without having to kill it. He might like, for example, to know how much central processor time it has already received. In some systems there is a difficulty in implementing facilities of this type, since the supervisor is being asked to do more than one thing for the same user at the same time.

Anything typed by the user thus goes either to the command interpreter (if he is in command status) or to the program that he is working with, unless it is preceded by the escape character when it is treated as an instruction to some part of the system and directed accordingly. The escape mechanism thus provides a unified way of meeting a number of requirements including local line editing, communicating with a running program, and passing requests to the supervisor while a program is running. An extension of the local line editing facility would be provision for invoking the system editor, or a simplified version of it, so that a user could make insertions or other changes to the line that he had just typed, instead of being restricted to cancelling the last character or the whole line.

3 **Process Management**

The processor in a time-sharing system divides its time between a variety of tasks. Some of these relate directly to the users' problems while others are performed under the authority of the supervisor. The latter may be divided into two categories. The first contains tasks that have to be performed regardless of time sharing, such as tasks concerned with input and output. The second contains tasks that are properly described as the private business of the supervisor and are concerned with such matters as time slicing, swapping, and the handling of interrupts. Tasks in the second category are part of the overheads that must be incurred in order that the benefits of time sharing shall be enjoyed.

If one looks at a multi-programmed or time-shared computer system in operation—and the points of this section are more clearly brought out if it is a system with more than one processor—then there are two ways in which one may follow what is going on. One may concentrate one's attention on a particular processor and observe the instructions that it is executing. As time goes on, and jumps of control take place, the processor will be executing first this procedure, then that procedure, and so on. One follows, as it were, the processor's 'stream of consciousness'. Alternatively, one may concentrate attention on the tasks—or *processes*, as they are usually called in this connection—that the system is charged with at a particular time. Some of these processes will be halted, while others will be free to run. Of those that are free to run, in all probability only a subset will be actually running, the number in the subset being equal to the number of processors. A process that is resumed after being halted does not necessarily run on the same processor that it was running on before.

If the processes were entirely independent, and if switching from one to the other were performed directly by the interrupt hardware, then these two points of view might, in the end, amount to very much the same thing, since, if a processor were executing a particular piece of code, it would be possible to say that it was running the process associated with that code. In fact, however, processes often share the use of procedures that exist in core in one copy only. In these circumstances, it is not possible to observe that a processor is running a particular section of code and to conclude that it is therefore running a particular process. The concept of a process is thus an abstract one, and may be compared with that of the life of an organism; in neither case is it very easy to pin the concept down in a definition.

Examples of routines that may be shared by a number of processes may be found in the supervisor. Suppose that a user's process needs to do some input or output; it will, for that purpose, enter an input or output routine belonging to the supervisor. In this case, since control will ultimately return to code indisputably belonging to the user, it is natural to regard the temporary entry into the supervisor as implying no change in the process. The process is said to run the supervisor routine as part of itself.

Another approach to the definition of what is meant by a process is to consider what information is needed to specify it. This must include:

(1) A starting, or restarting, address at which execution begins when the process is activated, or reactivated after being halted.

(2) A series of pointers to regions of core containing data.

(3) A series of pointers to regions of core that can be used as working space.

(4) An indication of the status of the process, that is whether it is free to run, halted, etc.

(5) For a halted process, information that must be loaded into the processor registers before the process is restarted.

In a formal sense, the totality of the above information may be said to constitute the process.

If there were no time-slicing, a process would be the path of the processor through the code. One may introduce the concept of a *virtual processor* that may be halted, but is not subject to interrupts. One can then regard a process as the path of such a virtual processor. This is perhaps one of the least confusing ways of looking at processes.

The word 'job' is ambiguous in relation to a time-sharing system. It was clear enough when all jobs were presented to a computer as a deck of punched cards and ended as another deck of punched cards or as printed output. The introduction of on-line consoles has posed a problem. The system designer is apt to regard a whole console session as a single job which, from time to time, receives input from the console and processes it. The console user, however, regards himself as creating a succession of jobs, the results of which come back to him; whenever the system reverts to command status and types the word READY, or the equivalent, he thinks of it as being ready to accept the next job. It is perhaps best to think of the user as owning a process that is, from time to time, halted and later reactivated. Each of these reactivations may correspond to the performance of a specific task.

At any given time, there will exist within the system under the management of the supervisor a variety of processes, some of which are system processes and some of which are processes belonging to object programs and known as OP processes. These processes will be arranged for convenience on a number of queues, some containing processes that are free to run and some containing processes that are halted for one reason or other, for example because they are waiting for some peripheral action to be completed. From time to time an OP process will need to perform an action for which it must make a call on the supervisor. Sometimes the supervisor can perform the necessary action unaided. On other occasions, it must establish and place on one of the queues of processes free to run a system process that will in due course complete the action. For example, a supervisor routine entered by an OP process for the purpose of printing a character will first place that character in a buffer and then queue a process that will, in due course, cause the character to be printed. In this case, the original process remains free to run, although whether it does so or not will depend on a decision taken by the supervisor; usually the supervisor will place it on one of the queues of halted processes and proceed to activate some other process, most likely the one that has just been queued.

Co-operating processes

Supervisor calls are needed whereby a process may halt itself or cause some other process to be halted or freed. These actions are sometimes referred to as *putting to sleep* and *waking up* respectively. The supervisor responds to these calls by placing the process concerned on the appropriate queue. Confusion would result if, before the supervisor had completed the execution of a call from process A affecting the status of process B, it were to accept a call from process C also affecting process B. This could happen if processes A and C were running on independent processors; it could also happen, if, as a result of an interrupt, process A were suspended and process C started. It is, therefore, essential that the supervisor should be designed so that calls of this nature appear to the calling process as indivisible or primitive operations; they are, in fact, often referred to as *primitives* and one speaks of issuing a primitive instead of making a supervisor call.

Similar situations occur whenever two or more processes are making a sequence of changes to the same area in memory. It is necessary that some form of interlocking should be provided whereby a process can, on reaching a critical point, lock out any other process until it has completed its updating operations. This may be achieved by using a word in memory to contain a *flag*. The flag is regarded as set or unset according as the word is equal to one or other of two arbitrarily selected quantities, for example, zero or one. When a process is about to make a change to the information in memory it first sets the flag. Any other process finding the flag set will itself refrain from initiating any similar action. Confusion of the type mentioned above can, however, occur if the testing of the flag and taking a decision involve the execution of more than one machine instruction. This problem can in its turn be avoided if the instruction set of the processor contains an instruction which enables the flag to be tested and set in one memory cycle. A suitable instruction is one which tests the content of a storage register and, if the content is found to be zero, sets it to some non-zero value; if the content is non-zero the instruction brings about a jump. Any instruction which changes the content of a storage register without destroying all the evidence of what was there before, can, however, be pressed into service; an example is an instruction which adds a number to a number in a storage register in one storage cycle. Such an instruction is a primitive at the hardware level.

While the use of flags provides, in principle, a solution to all synchronising problems, in practice their correct handling is far from easy and it is very difficult for the programmer to satisfy himself that his solution will work in all circumstances. Without realising it, he can easily create situations in which errors or deadlocks can

39

occur. Various writers have, therefore, proposed the provision of primitives which can be implemented with the aid of a flag-like mechanism and which provide more convenient tools for programmers to use. The best known and most successful of these are the P and V primitives of Dijkstra (1968); these operate on a non-negative integer called a *semaphore*. A semaphore may be regarded as a generalised flag. Definitions of P and V are as follows:

$P(s)$ **if** $s>0$ **then** $s:=s-1$ **else** halt process and place it on
                             a queue associated with s;

$V(s)$ $s:=s+1$;
        if queue not empty **then**
            begin $s:=s-1$;
                 remove a process from queue
                 and free it;
        end

A sequence of statements headed by $P(s)$ and terminated by $V(s)$ (with s set initially equal to one) constitutes a *critical region* and has the property that not more than one process may run in it at a time.

If used in a disciplined way, semaphores provide an elegant solution to most synchronisation problems. However, it is not easy for the programmer to satisfy himself that he has made no slip in their use and it is not possible to have the necessary checking carried out automatically by the compiler. There is, therefore, some interest in designing higher-level language constructs that could be implemented with the aid of semaphores or flags and put at the disposal of programmers. For a discussion of these the reader is referred to papers by Dijkstra, Brinch Hansen, Hoare, and others. References will be found in Brinch Hansen, 1973. The subject is one of great complexity. Apart from making it possible for the programmer to satisfy himself that his program is free from time-dependent errors and hence be able to certify it, the language constructs proposed must be capable of efficient implementation. In particular, situations must be avoided in which processes are repeatedly woken up only to be put to sleep again immediately because they are still unable to run.

Problems of synchronisation as distinct from mutual exclusion occur when two or more processes are co-operating on a common task. For example, one process may place information in a buffer ready for a second process to use. Such problems may be solved with

40

the aid of P and V primitives. An alternative approach is to make use of primitives of the type *cause event* and *await event*. Associated with the event is a message that is placed in a buffer and passed to the receiving process. An example of such an approach is found in the MULTICS system in which primitives of the above type have been used to implement a comprehensive interprocess communication facility that is available to the ordinary user as well as to system programmers (Spier and Organick, 1969).

The co-ordinator

The part of the supervisor that is responsible for setting up and administering the queues of processes that are free to run or halted will be known as the *co-ordinator*; this term, along with many ideas that are now familiar, was originally introduced by the designers of the Atlas supervisor (Kilburn *et al.*, 1961). An attempt will be made in this section to describe in outline the actions of a possible co-ordinator. It is not a description of any particular co-ordinator that has been implemented; in the design of co-ordinators, as of other software components, there is plenty of room for the exercise of private judgement on the part of the designer (see, for example, Bernstein *et al.*, 1969; Bétourné *et al.*, 1970).

The co-ordinator contains the necessary mechanism for putting processes on the various queues, for transferring them from one queue to another, and for taking a process from the queue of processes free to run and activating it. The co-ordinator comes into action as the result of one of three things happening. In the first place, an interrupt may occur coming from the clock or from a peripheral device. Secondly, there may be a trap caused, for example, by accumulator overflow, or by an attempt on the part of a process to access an area of core to which it is not entitled. Finally, a process may enter the co-ordinator voluntarily by making a supervisor call. When no process is free to run, the processor runs in an idling loop within the co-ordinator.

The queues that have been referred to are implemented as linked blocks of memory. Each process has associated with it a block known as the *process base*. This contains all necessary information about the process, including the starting or restarting address. It also contains pointers to the data and the working space that the process needs. If necessary, several blocks of data or working space can be linked to the process base by the use of techniques familiar in list processing. Process bases are joined to form a queue by means of a chain of pointers running through them. There are a number of free queues corresponding to different levels of priority. For example, when a process is running as part of itself a routine in the supervisor, then it may well be on a higher priority queue than otherwise. Again if a scheduling algorithm similar to that designed by Corbató for the CTSS (see p. 29) is used, then there may be a different queue corresponding to each level in the algorithm. There may similarly be a number of different halt queues, each corresponding to a different reason for the process being halted. At the cost of enlarging the process base to contain more pointers, provision may be made for a process to be on more than one queue at the same time. When a process that has just been running is placed on a halt queue, the contents of such processor registers as must be saved are stored in registers linked to the process base. If a process needs to run as part of itself a supervisor routine, it first attaches to its own process base all necessary information concerning that routine, including pointers to working space and data, together with a return link. It then enters the routine.

The interrupt routine may be regarded as part of the co-ordinator and is entered at arbitrary times by hardware action. The interrupt routine must first protect itself against further interrupts unless, indeed, this is done automatically by the hardware. It then determines the nature of the interrupt and enters an appropriate section of code. If servicing the interrupt is simple, then it can be performed directly by the interrupt routine. In general, however, the interrupt routine will queue a process that, in due course, will perform the task. As an example, consider interrupts coming from a clock at one millisecond intervals and suppose that there are a number of tasks to be performed every second and a number to be performed every minute. The interrupt routine keeps a count of the clock interrupts and ignores them unless they occur on the second or on the minute, in which case it queues a process that, when it comes to be run, will do what is necessary.

One of the reasons why only simple tasks are performed by the interrupt routine itself is that it is usually not safe to leave the interrupts turned off for more than a very limited period of time.

How long this is depends on the design of the hardware and, in particular, on what, if any, time-dependent peripherals are included in the system. An example of such a peripheral is a card reader that interrupts the computer as each column of holes comes up for reading; unless the computer responds appropriately, within a certain time, information will be lost. The existence of rigid deadlines of this type is fortunately not now common since peripherals that would otherwise give rise to them are usually connected through autonomous channels, or are provided with adequate buffering. However, the problem could become serious in the future if time-sharing systems come to be used to service real-time devices—experimental equipment, for example—that need to receive a response within a specified time. Apart from these considerations, however, an interrupt system cannot be expected to work satisfactorily unless interrupts are dealt with promptly. The trap routine can also be regarded as part of the co-ordinator and operates in a similar way.

Associated with the co-ordinator is a scheduling algorithm. This is consulted whenever an interrupt or a trap has taken place, or a running process has voluntarily entered the co-ordinator. The scheduling algorithm decides whether there shall be a change in process and, if so, which process shall be activated or reactivated. It is for the convenience of the scheduling algorithm that processes free to run are classified according to type and placed on a variety of queues rather than all being placed on the same queue.

Whenever the co-ordinator is entered, the processor is automatically switched to privileged mode. If the process activated by the co-ordinator is unprivileged, the co-ordinator will first set the memory protection limits appropriately, using for this purpose information about the process available in its own tables, together with information attached to the process base. It will then switch the processor to unprivileged mode before activating the process.

System tasks are, by their nature, short, and there is no point in delaying their execution. Accordingly, the co-ordinator will not activate an OP process unless there are no system processes free to run. When the co-ordinator is entered as a result of an interrupt or a trap, there will ordinarily be a process that was running when the interrupt took place, and the first decision to be taken by the scheduling algorithm is whether this process is to be reactivated or whether it is to be saved for reactivation later. Clearly, in view of the rule just stated, an interrupted OP process would give way to a waiting system process. Furthermore, the co-ordinator might discover that the interrupted OP process had exhausted its time slice and, indeed, the interrupt may have been one brought about by the clock in order that this determination might be made. On the other hand, unless some special reason exists to the contrary, it is likely that an interrupted system process will be resumed.

If there is no process on any of the queues of processes free to run, the co-ordinator enters an idling loop. It may be remarked in passing that the idling time need not be wholly wasted since it can be absorbed by the running of test programs; in particular, a test that the clock has not stopped may be found useful. Sooner or later the idling loop will be broken into by an interrupt, if only from the clock. The effect of the interrupt may be to put a new job on a free queue or to transfer a job from a halt queue to a free queue. The idling loop can be regarded as a process that has a lower priority than any other process and is always free to run.

The scheduling algorithm is also responsible for accepting jobs that have been presented to the system but have not so far been recognised by the co-ordinator. Some of these will be off-line or background jobs that in former days would have been kept on punched cards, or possibly on magnetic tape prepared off-line, until they were about to be run. Now they are queued within the system, having been read in by the supervisor and placed on the disc; active processing of them, however, has not yet begun. To these jobs must be added background jobs initiated from the foreground and queued in a similar way. Finally, there are on-line users wishing to log in and being offered to the scheduling algorithm by the logging in program.

In view of the varying status of new jobs awaiting attention, it is desirable to accommodate them on a number of separate queues (not to be confused with the queues administered by the co-ordinator that have just been discussed) according to their origin and priority. The design of that part of the scheduling algorithm that selects tasks from the various queues when the co-ordinator is ready to accept them is of critical importance. Not only must it give effect to the adopted policy in relation to the priority attaching to jobs in the various categories and to the proportion of processor time that is to be allocated to them, but it must ensure that the mix of accepted jobs is such as to keep all parts of the system in productive use as far as

44

that is possible. It is, for example, desirable that this mix should include one or more jobs that make use of magnetic-tape decks, and one or more that make heavy demands on the processor.

Handling of interrupts

One of the functions of the interrupt routine is to record information about the action to be taken when an expected interrupt occurs. This information must be provided by the process that initiates the action that will finally lead to the interrupt. For example, a process calling for a peripheral transfer might proceed to place itself on a halt queue, having indicated to the interrupt routine that it was to be transferred back to a free queue on the arrival of the interrupt indicating the completion of the transfer.

Some interrupts, however, must be referred to the owning process for a decision about action. These include interrupts that the writer of the program has foreseen and made arrangements for dealing with; they also include interrupts that arise as a result of a fault condition and whose occurrence is, therefore, unpredictable. If the process concerned is running when the interrupt occurs, no problem arises. If, however, the process is not running, then means must be provided whereby it is alerted to the interrupt as soon as it is next activated. This can be done by making the interrupt routine set a flag in the process base and attach thereto information about the nature of the interrupt. Before the co-ordinator activates a process it examines the flag to see whether or not there is an interrupt to be dealt with. An alternative is for the examination of the flag to be the responsibility of the process rather than that of the co-ordinator. The same mechanism can be used for passing information to a process about events that have occurred on a software, as distinct from a hardware, level. For example, if the user attempts to access a nonexistent file, then the file master (see Chapter 7) can cause the flag to be set and appropriate information to be provided.

Traps, which may be regarded as internally generated interrupts resulting from accumulator overflow, from an attempt to access a locked out part of memory, and from similar causes, are dealt with in the same way as external interrupts. It might be thought that, in the case of traps, the situation would be simpler in that the process concerned would be running when the trap occurred. However, many computers overlap the execution of instructions in order to gain additional speed. A trap may consequently occur after a jump has taken place and another process been entered.

The handling of interrupts and traps is one of the most complex areas of system programming. It covers the interface between hardware and software, and many problems, varying from computer to computer, must be faced. Apart from this, the system designer may set himself a more or less difficult task according to the standards of achievement at which he aims. For example, if he is content that all unexpected occurrences should lead to a user's program being aborted and information lost, then he will find life comparatively simple. If, however, he wishes to do his best for the user, to avoid aborting his program unless it is absolutely necessary, and, in any case, to provide him with detailed information about what has happened, then he sets himself a more exacting task. In some situations, for example when unexpected events occur in rapid succession, then it is probably best for the system to accept defeat; however, it should do this in such a way that as little harm as possible is done and as much information as possible is given to the user if it is a user's program that is concerned, or to the operating staff if it is a system program. The subject bristles with difficulties, and it is not surprising that, in the case of many operating systems, the design objectives have been unambitious.

Process saving

Information held in core memory may be dumped on to a drum with a view to future use for restarting purposes. One may distinguish between *physical dumps* and *logical dumps*. A physical dump is a straightforward record of the bit patterns as they exist in core without any regard to their meaning. A physical dump is sometimes referred to as a core image. When reloaded from a core image, core memory contains exactly the same bit pattern as it did originally. In a logical dump, on the other hand, the information content of core memory is recorded in a form that may bear no resemblance to the bit pattern, and indeed when the information is reloaded the bit pattern may be different. For example, in forming a logical dump of a list structure, the fact that one item contains a pointer to another would be recorded, but the actual addresses in which the two items were stored would not be recorded.

If an image of the whole core memory of a computer together with the contents of the processor registers (known as the processor *state words*) is dumped, then, on reloading, the computer is in exactly the same situation as it was when the dump took place, provided of course, that the contents of any discs or drums used as auxiliary memory are the same. Such a method of dumping is useful, for example, when circuits monitoring the supply mains have indicated that a supply failure is imminent.

A more common requirement in a time-sharing system is to be able to dump a single process. This was very simple in the CTSS, since there was only one segment of core memory associated with each user process, and this contained practically all the information needed for restarting the process. It was thus quite easy to provide a command that would save, in a file, a user's core image together with the other information needed for re-starting, and a corresponding command that would enable him to resume his work at any time in the future at exactly the point at which he broke off. Apart from its obvious uses, this feature enabled the system to save a user's status automatically whenever it was necessary to log him out forcibly, for example, when he had exhausted his time allocation for the current session. The SAVE and RESUME commands also provided a means whereby a user could create a personal command in a particularly simple manner.

In more modern time-sharing systems, it is not sufficient to dump the core areas used by a process to hold its program and data; it is also necessary to dump the information associated with the process base. The former information can readily be dumped in physical form, but the latter is usually held as part of a linked data structure in core space administered by the supervisor. If information relating to one process only is to be dumped, that information must be extracted from the data structure and dumped in logical form. For this reason it is not a trivial matter to provide save and resume facilities that extend from one session to another. There is no difficulty, however, in providing a facility whereby a user may examine the core image of a suspended program and then, if necessary, restart it after patching. While he is doing this the information held in his process base remains

47

intact. As soon, however, as he logs-out, or activates another program, this information, being held in core memory, is destroyed and the interrupted process is irrevocably lost.

Sub-processes

As far as a co-ordinator is concerned, all the processes that it controls are on a single level and it administers them with a single set of queues. Any relationships that exist between the processes—for example, that D and E are sub-processes of A—are recorded separately in a table which, along with tables containing other administrative information, may be consulted by the scheduling algorithm. For example, if both A and D are free to run and E is not free to run then A and D will both be on the (same) run queue and E will be on the wait queue. The scheduling algorithm will take account of the fact that D and E are sub-processes of A; for example, it may never allow A to run if either D or E is free. Similarly the system routine whose function is to delete processes no longer required, would, if asked to delete A, also delete D and E. Fig. 3.1, taken from a paper by Brinch Hansen (1970) illustrates this point of view. The tree of processes is merely a way of exhibiting diagrammatically the relationships recorded in the table.

In some circumstances, as will be explained shortly, one co-

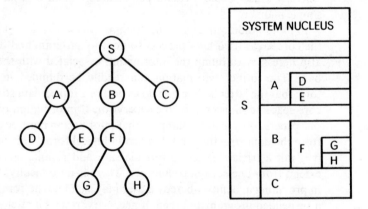

Fig. 3.1 One view of sub-processes

ordinator may operate under another, or there may be a series of co-ordinators forming a hierarchy. Fig. 3.2 shows such an arrangement. A situation of this kind leads to a very different view of sub-processes. In the diagram the top level co-ordinator is responsible for three processes 1, 2, and 3. Process 1 when running in a lower-level co-ordinator gives rise to sub-processes 1.1 and 1.2; similarly for process 3 which gives rise to the sub-processes 3.1, 3.2, and 3.3. The top-level co-ordinator, however, has no knowledge of these sub-processes. When from the point of view of the lower co-ordinator sub-process 1.1 is running, as seen by the top-level co-ordinator it is process 1 that is running. Fig. 3.2 is essentially a flow diagram in that it traces the flow of control of a process through the various procedures, some of which may be co-ordinators, in which it runs. Fig. 3.2 thus differs radically from Fig. 3.1 which is a purely diagrammatic way of exhibiting relationships. It is not, however, to be implied that there is anything incompatible between the two ways of implementing sub-processes and it is perfectly possible for them to exist side by side in the same system.

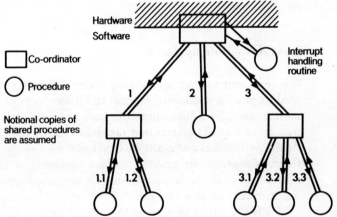

Fig. 3.2 Another view of sub-processes. The top co-ordinator is partly in the hardware.

It may be noted that the first way of implementing sub-processes does not favour any particular policy as regards scheduling. The use of cascaded co-ordinators on the other hand does imply a particular policy, namely, that a process may create sub-processes, but may not

49

thereby gain access to additional computer resources, since it must share those that it has been allocated with the subsidiary processes that it creates. Since a process can never be allocated more than one processor by the top co-ordinator, it follows that lower-level co-ordinators can never have more than one processor at their disposal. This is true of all systems known to me in which one co-ordinator runs under another.

The policy described in the last paragraph is the appropriate one to adopt in many circumstances, particularly when it is desired to allocate a fixed proportion of the available resources to a subsystem or to a group of users. In other circumstances, however, an exactly opposite policy may be adopted. The specific object of allowing processes to create subsidiary processes may be to allow a particularly large and important job to secure the temporary use of a large part of the total resources available and thus to be able to run more quickly in real time. This is likely to be the point of view of owners of large systems in which several processors are provided with the express object of securing speed through the exploitation of parallel working.

Systems within systems

Self-contained subsystems running under the main system may be used to provide specialised services to on-line users or to a class of on-line users. Such subsystems can vary widely in their characteristics. The FIGARO system that ran under the Cambridge Multiple-Access System was one example. Other examples are provided by the *transaction processing systems* that are becoming of increasing importance in business data processing for such applications as invoicing, inventory control, and so on.

Ideally the writer of a subsystem should have at his disposal the same facilities—including facilities for memory protection—as did the writer of the original system. He would then be able, within the resources of processor time and memory space allocated to him, to write an operating system with which he could, as it were, set up a private computing service on his own. In particular, he would be able to protect his operating system from corruption by the users working under it. One can go further and envisage a hierarchy of levels of

50

indefinite depth at each of which full facilities for writing private and protected subsystems are available. Whether or not there is an operational requirement for this capability in its extreme form, discussion of the extent to which it can or cannot be provided is a touchstone for testing the generality and elegance of any particular design for an operating system. It is perhaps in relation to memory protection that the most progress remains to be made. The problem in a conventional computer is that, whereas the main co-ordinator can run in privileged mode, any lower-level co-ordinators written by ordinary users must run in non-privileged mode. Unless special steps are taken, therefore, in the design of the main system, no protection can be given to lower-level co-ordinators. The subject of protection is discussed in greater details in Chapter 4.

In a hierarchical system each co-ordinator runs under the control of the co-ordinator above it. In other words a co-ordinator must be thought of as being outside the universe that it controls. A difficulty arises at the top of the hierarchy since there is no superior co-ordinator to which the top co-ordinator can be responsible. A solution to this problem is found in recognising that at the top-level co-ordination is partly performed by the hardware; one can either say that a primitive co-ordinator is built into the hardware or that the top-level co-ordinator is partly implemented in hardware and partly implemented in software. It is at this top level that the traps and interrupts generated within the hardware are initially processed; when necessary they are passed down in software guise through the hierarchy. The top-level co-ordinator thus differs in an essential manner from lower-level co-ordinators.

4　Memory addressing and protection

This chapter is concerned with the memory addressing and protection facilities required for the efficient multi-programming of object programs. The early systems described in Chapter 2 depended on simple swapping; that is, there was only one object program in core at once. Simple swapping undoubtedly makes for simplicity in the supervisor, since scheduling, although by no means a trivial matter, is concerned only with the allocation of the processor, there being no core allocation problem.

If drums have to be used, there is little doubt that the long swapping time will make simple swapping uneconomic in future. A few years ago it appeared possible that there might become available mass core or mass LSI memories of comparable size and cost to high-speed drums. How such memories would have been used is a matter for speculation. System designers would hardly have been content, in the long term, to use a random access device—if, indeed, the mass memories had had that property—as a direct replacement for a drum, which is essentially a serial access device. Possibly, slaving techniques, using a normal-sized high-speed memory as the slave, would have been developed. (Wilkes, 1965.) We may still see developments in the use of large non-rotating memories of intermediate speed, but current progress in semiconductor technology seems rather to be leading in the direction of very large memories with speeds little if at all inferior to those of present-day high-speed memories.

Multi-programming

If multi-programming of object programs is to be possible, a sufficiently large high-speed memory must be provided; ideally, there should be sufficient space to accommodate two or three of the largest programs it is desired to run under the system. Since under multi-programming, a given object program does not always get loaded into the same place in core, it is necessary to have a hardware relocation register or *base register*, whose contents are added automatically to the memory register address before the memory is accessed. Whenever a program is activated, the memory address in which it starts is loaded into the base register by the supervisor. Associated with the base register is a *limit register* used to give memory protection; this is also loaded by the supervisor when a program is activated.

Generally, in a multi-programming system, it will be desired to make use of *pure procedures*, that is procedures which do not themselves change and which can work as subroutines for more than one object program at the same time. Since a pure procedure must have separate working space for each program for which it is acting as a subroutine, efficient implementation requires that there should be a second base register, with its associated limit register. Additional pairs of base and limit registers may be provided with advantage. A pure procedure can be activated freely on behalf of any program authorised to use it, but it must not be modified. Data, also, must sometimes be protected from accidental corruption. We are thus led to demand a memory protection system which distinguishes between reading and writing, that is, which allows a part of the store to be read from but not written into. A further refinement is to be able to allow the contents of a section of memory to be executed as code, but not read or over-written.

Paging and segmentation

Paging

Paging is a more elaborate way of organising a core memory that gives, at the cost of some hardware complication, a number of advantages not obtainable with simple base registers. The digits giving the address of a word in memory are divided into two sections; the more significant digits are regarded as determining the *page number*, and the least significant digits as determining the line in the page. The effect of this is to divide a program or block of data into sections known as *pages*. The core memory is similarly divided into *page frames*, each capable of taking one page of a program or block of data. Since consecutive pages of program do not, when loaded into core memory, necessarily go into consecutive page frames, the supervisor must form a *page table*, giving the page frame into which each page of program or data has gone. The page table must be kept up to date as changes are made in the contents of the core memory.

When a word is to be accessed, the page number in the address is split off and used to enter the page table. The page table gives the relevant page frame number, and this number, with the line number appended, is the physical address of the required word in the memory. More formally, this may be expressed as follows: let p be the page number and l the line number so that a complete memory address is $2^\alpha p + l$, where 2^α is the number of lines in a page. If the page table is stored as a one-dimensional array (in the ALGOL sense) denoted by P, then the physical address in the core store is $2^\alpha P[p] + l$. The access cycle just described is performed automatically, and the programmer need have no knowledge of what is going on. This is sometimes expressed by saying that paging is transparent to the programmer.

If the page table were kept in core, a severe time penalty would be incurred since two core cycles instead of one would be required to obtain a word from memory, one cycle to access the page table, and one to obtain the required word. However, the number of registers needed for the page table is not large, and it is practicable to provide fast hardware registers for the purpose. If this is done, only a slight slowing down of the computer need be accepted. The scheme is shown diagrammatically in Fig. 4.1, and may be referred to as *direct paging*.

In a multiple-access multi-programmed system, the use of paging gives a number of advantages. In the first place, when a fresh program comes to be loaded, it can go into any page frames which can be made available, whether or not they are consecutive. Secondly, paging allows traffic in the channel between the drum and the core memory to be reduced, since a page of program need not be loaded until it is actually needed. This is sometimes called *demand paging*. The procedure is to load the first page of a program and send control to it. If, in due course, an attempt is made to access a word in another page, a trap occurs; the supervisor is entered, loads the required page, and updates the page table. Since, in multiple-access working, programs are often loaded and run for short periods only (until they reach an input or output wait, or have exhausted their quantum of time), this advantage of paging is an important one. A further reduction in traffic can be obtained if, associated with each page register,

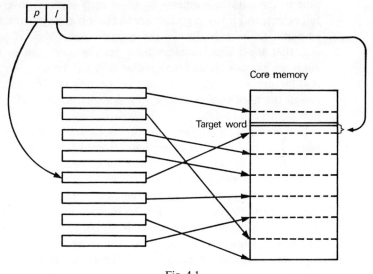

Fig. 4.1

there is a bit which is originally zero and becomes set to one the first time the page is written into. The supervisor can then avoid writing back on to the drum pages which have not been altered during their residence in core. Memory protection can be associated with pages if extra bits associated with the page registers are provided for the purpose.

Segments

A program ordinarily comprises a main routine, some subroutines, and one or more sections of data. Each of these separate items is known as a *segment*, and has its own scheme of numbering of registers, starting from zero and going up. The technique was early introduced of assembling the various segments of a program automatically by means of an assembly program, or linking loader, which performs the functions of memory space allocation and address modification. In this system, address parameters left undefined by the programmer are fixed or *bound* at loading time. This has the dis-

55

advantage that enough memory space must be allocated at assembly time to the various segments to allow each segment to grow to its full extent, and if two segments are to share memory space, this must be explicitly allowed for by the programmer. While it cannot be said that these disadvantages have been severely felt in the past, many people are of the opinion that they will be more serious now that large multiple-access systems are coming in. The solution is to design the hardware in such a way that the binding of the address parameters can be deferred until run time.

It is necessary that there should be further digits in a memory address to the left of the page digits; these digits define the *segment number*. At run time, the segment number is used to enter the *segment table* belonging to the user whose program is running at that instant. The segment table gives the address of the base of another table, namely the page table, for the segment in question. This table is entered using the page number from the memory address as an index. The page table finally yields the number of the page frame, and this with the line number appended gives the physical address.

The segment and page tables are to be thought of as permanently resident in core memory when the user's program is running.

The segment tables corresponding to the various users are stored in core memory, and there is a hardware register which is loaded by the supervisor with the address of the base of the segment table belonging to the user whose program is currently active. This number is added to the segment number and used to enter the segment table. This explanation may be expressed more concisely as follows: let s be the segment number, so that the complete memory address may be written $(2^\beta s + p)\, 2^a + l$, where β is the number of page digits. If S is the segment table and u is the number in the special hardware register referred to above, then the physical address accessed in the memory is

$$2^a P[S[s+u]+p]+l.$$

As the pages are loaded into core, or dumped on to the drum, the page table must be updated. Each user must have a segment table, but there need be only one page table for each segment in use, since, if two users are using the same segment, their respective segment tables can both contain pointers to the same page table.

Associative memory

Without a further addition to the hardware, the system just described would not be workable since three memory cycles instead of one would be needed for each word accessed. The solution that has been arrived at is to provide an associative memory constructed from very fast registers which will enable the access procedure just described to be short-circuited on the great majority of occasions. The associative memory contains number pairs consisting of the segment and page numbers from an address, combined to form a single number, and the corresponding page frame number. Thus, in the notation used above, the associative memory receives the following pair of numbers: $2^{\beta}s + p$; $P[S[s + u] + p]$. Whenever a memory access is to be made, the associative memory is interrogated to ascertain whether it contains an entry corresponding to the combined segment and page numbers from the address in question. If it does, then the associative memory yields at once the number of the required page frame. The line number is appended and an access to the core memory initiated. Thus, instead of three core memory cycles, we have one interrogation of the associative memory, which can be made extremely rapid, and only one core access cycle, so that the total access time is very little in excess of that required in a conventional computer. If the associative memory does not contain the required information, then the full procedure involving three memory cycles is gone through. The connection between the segment and page specified in the instruction and the page frame in core memory having now been established, an appropriate entry is made in the associative memory so that the next time an access is required to that page the full procedure can be short-circuited.

Considerations of cost make it impossible for the associative memory to contain many registers, and the number that has been adopted in current designs is either eight or sixteen. Unless the associative memory has very recently been cleared, it will be necessary to suppress an item of information in order to make room for a new one; the obvious thing is to suppress the item that has been there for the longest period of time, but other algorithms slightly cheaper to implement have also been proposed. Schroeder (1971) has reported that in the MULTICS system sixteen associative registers enable the full procedure of three memory cycles to be short-circuited on more than 98

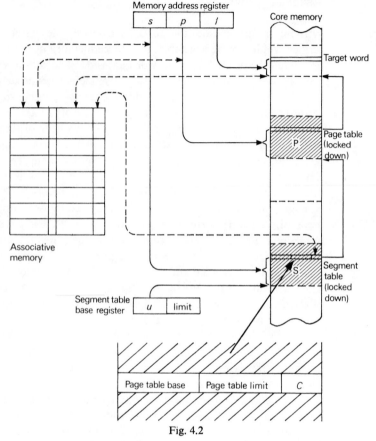

Fig. 4.2

per cent of occasions. Those who prefer to have things explained with a diagram are referred to Fig. 4.2.

Paging algorithm

There is no difficulty about arranging that pages should be loaded only when they are required. There is, however, more difficulty in arriving at a satisfactory algorithm for deciding which page should be dumped when it is necessary to make room for an incoming page. One policy is to dump the page that has been longest resident in core without being accessed. More elaborate criteria, based on the past history of all pages in core, may be constructed and the matter is discussed in detail in the next chapter.

The set of segment tables for all processes known to the supervisor form a segment which will be called the *segment-table segment*, and which may run to several pages in length. Only those pages which contain information relating to processes actually in run status need to be loaded in core. There is, thus, a paging problem in relation to the segment-table segment. This cannot be handled by the normal algorithm, since the access cycle as described above will not work unless both segment and page tables are already loaded. Moreover, the supervisor knows exactly when and for what periods a segment table is required to be in memory, and can therefore handle the matter without difficulty. It may be helpful to give an outline of the sequence of events that take place when a process returns to working status after a gap; this is as follows:

(1) The page of the segment-table segment containing the segment table in question is loaded (if it is not already in core).

(2) The entries in the segment table are adjusted to point to the page tables of any segments that are also being used by other processes already in working status and which, therefore, have page tables in core. A counter associated with each such page table is increased by one.

(3) Page tables are created for those segments which do not already have them, and the counters are set to one. This action can be deferred until the first page is loaded.

(4) As pages are loaded or unloaded by the paging algorithm, the entries in the corresponding page tables are set or cancelled.

When the process goes out of working status, the relevant page of the segment-table segment is unloaded, unless it also contains the segment table for some process still in working status. In any case, the counters associated with all page tables to which it refers are reduced by one. Page tables whose counters are zero are abandoned, and the space they occupy, together with the space occupied by any pages to which they point, is made available for re-use.

Safeguards must be incorporated in order to prevent a user's program getting access to segment or page tables with which it has no business. If the hardware register which contains the base of the user's segment table is made long enough to contain also the length of the segment table, a check may be made that the segment number in the instruction is a valid one. Similarly, the segment table may be made to yield not only the page table base for that segment but also the length of the page table. Complete memory protection may be obtained by adding to the entries in the segment table two extra digits—C in Fig. 4.2—to indicate the class of access permitted, that is, read only, read and write, or execute only. The associative memory must be extended so that these digits can be stored when a page is first accessed and delivered up, along with the page frame number, whenever the associative memory is later interrogated successfully.

Some implementations provide for the access-class digits to be associated with page frames, and set when a page is loaded; however the same segment may be used with different classes of access by two or more processes, and it would appear to be more logical to associate class with a segment table. The subject of memory protection is taken up again in more detail on p. 65.

Note that, in the system just described, the page tables (one for each segment) are located in core memory, whereas, in the earlier rather different system which provided paging only, it was necessary to have a set of rapid-access page registers. On the other hand, the segmentation system requires for its practical implementation that there should be an associative memory of at least eight registers. The cost of the segmentation system is not necessarily very much greater than that of a simple paging system.

If the segment number, page number, and line number are thought of as forming a single numerical address, then the various segments can be regarded as being held in a very large *virtual memory*. The fact that this memory is very large, compared with the lengths of the various segments that are held in it, means that there can be big gaps between the segments, and it is this that allows the segments to grow dynamically. Since the memory is virtual and not real, these gaps do not correspond to anything physically present either in core or on the drum.

Historical note

The virtual memory concept, according to which the program space is much larger than the physical core space, is made possible by the use of the associative memory. It would not be made possible by a scheme such as that shown in Fig. 4.1 in which the (hardware) page registers are addressed directly; this is because of the large number of such registers that would be required, namely, one for each page in the program space. If, however, the page registers are designed to be accessed associatively, there can be fewer of them, and the virtual memory concept at once becomes possible. This was first done in the Atlas computer, designed by T. Kilburn and his colleagues who were responsible for introducing these ideas into computer technology. The core memory of the Atlas computer was, by modern standards, small, and sufficient associative paging registers were provided to cater for all the pages that could be held in core at any one time. These registers were loaded directly by the supervisor. In the more recently designed systems, there are far fewer associative registers than there are pages in core, and there is provision for loading them automatically in the way that has been described.

For early papers on segmentation and the design of computer systems in which run time binding of segments could take place, the reader is referred to the publications of Dennis and Van Horn (see References). A paper by Arden, Galler, O'Brien and Westervelt (1966) is also of interest. The first computer to be designed with a memory access system along the lines of Fig. 4.2 was the GE645 developed for the MULTICS project at Project MAC, M.I.T. (Corbató and Vyssotsky, 1965; Organick, 1972). This was followed shortly afterwards by the IBM 360/67. The description given above may be misleading in relation to these two computers unless it is explained that the address shown as existing in the memory address register of Fig. 4.2 is not the quantity that occurs in the address field of the instruction, but is formed from that quantity by the addition of the number in a selected base register. Indexing may take place as well. The base register to be used is indicated by a tag of three or four bits in the instruction. It is important to note that, since the address field in the instruction does not contain the full number of digits needed for the constructed address, the segment digits, s, are, in fact, supplied from the base register. Thus a more detailed version of Fig. 4.2 would show the base register tag (segment tag in MULTICS nomenclature) in an instruction pointing to a base register, whose more significant digits point to the relevant entry in the segment table.

Details differ in the two computers, and for these and the corresponding software conventions, the reader is referred to the relevant publications (Daley and Dennis, 1968; IBM, 1966).

Swapping and the virtual memory concept

In a system without a virtual memory, programs are read into core from the files containing them when the programs are first loaded; data files remain on the disc or drum and are accessed in the ordinary way. Some space on the drum is set aside for swapping and, when a user's quantum of time is exhausted, his program is transferred from core to the drum. Later, when that user's turn comes up again, the program will be reloaded. Thus, at any time, a given user's program is either in core or exists on the drum as a core image. When the program eventually becomes dead or dormant, the core image still exists on the drum; eventually it will be replaced by the next program activated by that user. Until this occurs, however, the program is available for post-mortem examination or reactivation and can, if the user wishes be filed away for future use by means of a SAVE command.

Given a virtual memory there are two possibilities. One is to copy program files and short data files into the virtual memory and to access other data files through system buffers as is done in non-virtual memory systems. The other is to embody all files as they stand into the virtual memory. This is often expressed by saying that the files are *attached* to the virtual memory.

If the first method is used the user's program and data on the drum correspond very closely to a core image, except that they can in aggregate amount to many more words than the core could accommodate. The paging system is responsible for bringing into core those pages that are required at any particular time and, even if all the pages would go into core, it is very unlikely that they will all be there at once.

In the second system, a file is not copied but is simply renamed as a segment; for example, the file ADAM might become segment number 55. Nothing changes except for an entry being made in a table. If the user refers in his program to a particular word in segment 55 then the page containing that word will be loaded by the paging system. If the contents of a page are changed while the page is in core, then the revised version will, in due course, be copied back on to the drum or disc to replace the original one. Thus, permanent changes may be made in a file while that file is attached to a user's virtual memory. If the user wishes to be sure of preserving the contents of a file—other than a read-only file—in their original form, he must make a copy before he attaches the file to the virtual memory.

An operating system designed for a computer with a virtual memory consists of (1) a certain amount of code and data locked down in core and responsible for loading pages, controlling the drums and discs, etc., and (2) code and data brought into core as required by the paging system. The latter do not differ in any way from code and data belonging to user's programs, except that they may enjoy a higher degree of protection.

Each user on being logged-in is presented with a virtual memory for his own use. Into it are already loaded the code and data segments just mentioned. For example, in the Edinburgh Multiple Access System (EMAS) (Whitfield and Wight 1973) a virtual memory consists of 256 segments each of 2^{16} bytes. Segments 0–31 of each virtual memory are preloaded with system routines or data. The rest are available to the user. In this context the term 'user' may indicate the writer of a subsystem. The ordinary user of a high-level language will not be aware of segments or segment numbers, since all this will have been taken care of by the writer of the language subsystem that he is using. In MULTICS segments are known by their full alphanumeric names even to the writers of subsystems. Internally they are, of course, numbered, but the numbers are allocated quite automatically by the system and the user knows nothing of them.

Segment loading and inter-segment linking in MULTICS

For each process, the MULTICS supervisor maintains a *known segment table* which is, in effect, an index connecting the alphanumeric names of segments with the segment numbers currently associated with them. If a segment is represented in the known segment table, it may be said to be *loaded*. The operation of loading a new segment, that is, of adding an appropriate entry to the segment table and updating the known segment table, is performed by the *segment loader*. This operation would normally take place at runtime when the first reference to a segment is encountered. The fact that a segment is loaded in the sense of being represented in the known segment table does not, of course, imply that any particular page will be resident in core; it is, however, the duty of the paging algorithm to load any page of such a segment when that page is called for.

Cross-references from one segment to another are very common. For example, a procedure segment written in an assembly language—the example could equally well be in some higher level language—might contain the following statement:

$$CLA \quad ADAM \quad PLACE \; + \; 4$$

where ADAM is the name of some other segment, and PLACE is a label within that segment. In a conventional computing system, the identifiers ADAM and PLACE would be replaced by their numerical values when the process was loaded. This would, however, be quite contrary to the spirit of segmentation, which is to defer any form of linkage as long as possible. The use of a loader would, moreover, only be satisfactory if it were known in advance that certain segments, and those segments only, constituted the process, and that all the segments would be used. In practice, some segments, for example segments dealing with errors or unexpected conditions, may not, in fact, be invoked at all, while, on the other hand, a user at a console may very well type a command which will require the attachment of some hitherto unmentioned segment to his program. For these reasons, it is better that the establishment of inter-segmental links should be deferred to runtime, and that any particular link should not be established until it is actually needed. The first system of this kind was conceived for the MULTICS project. The principle adopted is to have a *linking routine* which is called into action whenever an attempt is made to use a link for the first time and which establishes the link for use then and on subsequent occasions; if necessary, it calls on the segment loader to load the called segment.

There are, however, complications associated with the use of pure procedures that rule out the establishment of direct links. In the first place, a pure procedure should remain inviolate and not have a reference to another procedure planted into it. In the second place, a pure procedure that has been loaded may be serving more than one process, and it could obviously not be linked directly to all of them at the same time. The answer lies in some form of indirect addressing.

In MULTICS, each procedure segment has associated with it a *linkage segment* which is created by the assembler or compiler that produced the procedure segment itself. References to external segments are compiled as references to points in the linkage segment. Initially, the linkage segment contains at each of these points a word that will cause a trap the first time an attempt is made to use the link; it also contains the symbolic name of the referenced segment and the point of entry. As a result of the trap, the linking routine is activated and plants a reference to the called segment into the linkage segment, overwriting the word that caused the trap. The called segment can now be accessed as required and, on subsequent occasions, the whole operation of accessing the segment goes quite smoothly, allowing of course for the fact that there may be a paging trap. If a pure procedure is working for more than one process, then a separate copy of the linkage segment must be made for each process; note that the original linkage segment is preserved in the filing system, and that the copies used by the processes are ultimately thrown away.

The objection to the system just described is that every reference from one segment to another involves an extra memory access. There appears to be no way, however, of avoiding the need for an indirect reference if the requirement for pure procedures is to be met. One can, however, avoid the extra memory access by using hardware registers for the indirect addressing. Suitable registers do, in fact, exist on the GE645 computer for which MULTICS has been implemented (see p. 61), and there is the option of using them for matrix manipulating procedures and other cases where time is critical.

Hardware for memory protection

The hardware feature that makes it possible to design a time-sharing system so that a user program cannot interfere with any part of the supervisor, or with any other user program, is memory protection. In earlier computers with no memory protection the only way open to the system designer to secure safe operation was to write his system so as to run interpretively. Systems programmers now demand that it should be possible to lockout all memory except that between narrowly controlled limits and that, within those limits, it should be possible to specify that access should be any one of the following: (1) read only, (2) read and write, (3) execute as program. A segment with the last class of access may be run as a program but may not be used as a data segment for either reading or writing by another program. It is convenient, however, if means are provided whereby an execute only segment can read data words (constants) from itself. Execute only access is clearly useful in cases where it is desired to give customers the use of a program but not to allow them to print a copy, although the same effect can be obtained by other means; it is also useful when programs are being debugged as a means of ensuring that overwriting of pure procedures does not take place.

One may distinguish two different approaches to the problem of protection. As an example in another field, consider the case of a public library which needs a system for controlling admission and for the issuing of books to authorised borrowers. One method of controlling admission is for the door-keeper to be provided with a list of authorised users of the library. Anyone seeking admission is then asked to state and prove his identity, after which, if his name is on the list, he is allowed to enter. In the alternative system, users are provided with tickets of admission which, when exhibited to the door-keeper, gain them the right to enter. Similarly, borrowing can be controlled either by a list kept by the library clerk or by providing borrowers with a written authorisation in the form of a ticket. Note that on the former system authorisation is passed from the controlling authority to the facility and that, on the second system, the authorisation is passed from the controlling authority to the user.

In order to illustrate how ideas and practice relating to memory protection have developed, I shall describe an evolutionary series of possible computer organisations. The series is evolutionary in the sense that it illustrates the organic relationship of one scheme to another, and I do not mean to imply that development actually took place in the way suggested. Readers who are familiar with the organisation of particular machines will be able to form their own judgement as to the relationship, if any, these organisations bear to the canonical series here described.

To begin with, it will be assumed that the computer has core memory only, and it may help to think of it as being a very large core memory. In order to simplify the argument as much as possible there is no reference to index registers, which can, however, be added without difficulty in all cases. The execution sequences given are for instructions, such as addition and subtraction, which involve an operand access to the memory.

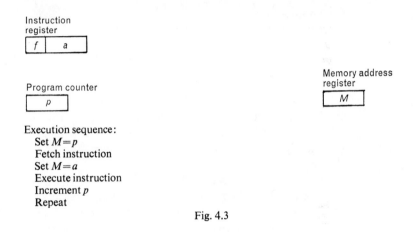

Instruction register

| f | a |

Program counter

| p |

Memory address register

| M |

Execution sequence:
  Set $M = p$
  Fetch instruction
  Set $M = a$
  Execute instruction
  Increment p
  Repeat

Fig. 4.3

Fig. 4.3 shows a primitive machine organisation in which no memory protection of any kind is provided. Fig. 4.4 shows a simple form of protection in which there is a single double-length register in which two numbers, the *base* and *limit* respectively, can be placed. These numbers define the limits within which the memory may be accessed when the computer is running in its normal mode; note that the base register is also used for relocation. There must be a privileged mode in which protection does not operate and in which the base-limit register can be loaded. This is indicated in the figure by showing a flip-flop which, when set, switches the computer to privileged mode. If the execution sequence is followed, it will be seen that the address in the program counter is first checked to make sure that it is within range. If not, a trap occurs, and control is sent to a fixed absolute register in memory; the content of the program counter is saved. If no trap occurs, the instruction is fetched, and the address in it tested to see whether it is within range. If not, a trap occurs as before, but

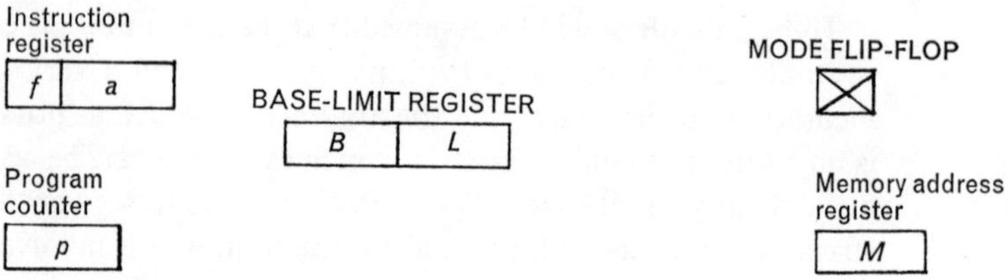

Instruction
register

f	a

BASE-LIMIT REGISTER

B	L

MODE FLIP-FLOP

⊠

Program
counter

p

Memory address
register

M

Execution sequence:
  Set $M = B + p$ if $p \leqslant L$; otherwise trap
  Fetch instruction
  Set $M = B + a$ if $a \leqslant L$; otherwise trap
  Execute instruction
  Increment p
  Repeat
Trap sets mode flip-flop

Fig. 4.4

if all is well, execution of the order is completed. On the occurrence of a trap, the privileged mode flip-flop is set, and remains set until it is explicitly reset by an instruction in the trap routine or elsewhere in the supervisor.

The system of protection shown in Fig. 4.4 is based on the presumption that program and data will be all together in a continuous block of storage. Fig. 4.5 shows a more complicated system in which it is possible to have two separated blocks, one containing program and one containing data; in other words, the program may consist of

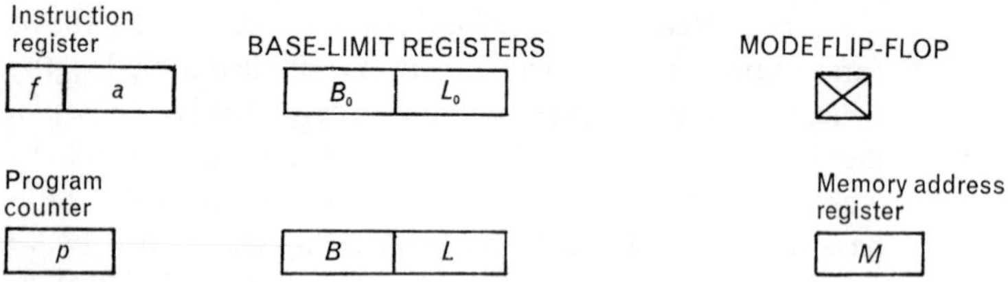

Instruction
register

f	a

BASE-LIMIT REGISTERS

B_0	L_0

MODE FLIP-FLOP

⊠

Program
counter

p

B	L

Memory address
register

M

Execution sequence:
  Set $M = B + p$ if $p \leqslant L$; otherwise trap
  Fetch instruction
  Set $M = B_0 + a$ if $a \leqslant L_0$; otherwise trap
  Execute instruction
  Increment p
  Repeat
Trap sets mode flip-flop

Fig. 4.5

two distinct segments. There are two base-limit registers, one used for relocating and checking the validity of the operand address, and one used for relocating and checking the validity of the address in the program counter. The execution sequence of a typical instruction is otherwise as before; in particular, there is a normal mode of operation and a privileged mode entered when a trap occurs. The content of the base-limit register, regarded as a single register, may be termed a *segment descriptor*. For each segment within its cognizance, the supervisor has, among other information, a segment descriptor, and this is loaded into one of the base-limit registers when the segment is about to be used.

Fig. 4.6 shows a further elaboration of the system of protection in which the number of base-limit registers has been increased above two. One of these is still associated exclusively with the program counter, but any of the others may be used for relocating and checking the validity of an operand address. Which register is used is determined by a segment number that forms part of the address.

It becomes profitable at this point to introduce classes of protection, and the base-limit registers are shown as having an extra section marked *C*, which has space for two bits. According to the content of *C*, certain instructions are enabled or disabled. This is indicated in the figure by showing a series of flip-flops called *enabling flip-flops*. During the execution of an instruction, some of these flip-flops will become set and the corresponding functions enabled; if, later, it is found that the instruction calls for some function that has not been enabled, a trap occurs. When the instruction is completed, all the enabling flip-flops are re-set to their original condition. In the scheme of Fig. 4.6, *C* can have the values R, RW, or E. It will be seen from the table appended to the figure that R sets the read enabling flip-flop only, while RW sets both the read enabling and the write enabling flip-flops. It is thus possible to have some segments which are read only, and some which can be written into as well. Neither of the enabling flip-flops is set by E, and a trap will occur if an attempt is made to read an operand from such a segment, or to write one into it. A program contained in such a segment may, however, be executed if the segment descriptor is placed in the base-limit register associated with the program counter.

This system of protection is very powerful. By keeping a stock of segment descriptors for the various segments under its control, the supervisor can authorise an object program to make use of a particular segment in a suitably restricted or unrestricted manner. If an object program has occasion to use a system program, it must appeal to the supervisor, which will ascertain whether or not it is authorised to do so. If it is authorised, the supervisor will load the necessary descriptors into the base-limit registers.

So far it has been assumed that there is a one-level physical core memory. A virtual memory may be substituted for the latter with no

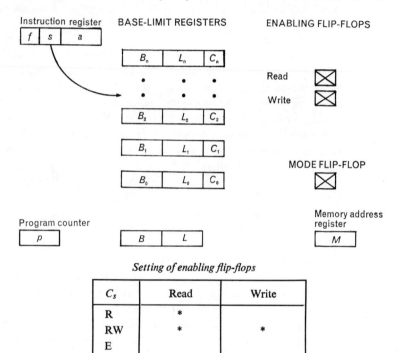

Setting of enabling flip-flops

C_s	Read	Write
R	*	
RW	*	*
E		

Execution sequence:
 Set $M = B + p$ if $p \leqslant L$; otherwise trap
 Fetch instruction into instruction register
 Set enabling flip-flops from C_s
 Set $M = B_s + a$ if $a \leqslant L_s$; otherwise trap
 Execute instruction; trap if execution not enabled
 Increment p
 Repeat
Trap sets mode flip-flop

Fig. 4.6

70

other change in the system. For example, the memory address register of Fig. 4.6 could be identified with the memory address register of Fig. 4.2. This, however, would result in unnecessary duplication, since the virtual memory system of Fig. 4.2 itself already contains a full protection system. If the entries in the segment table in Fig. 4.2 are regarded as being the (software) equivalents of the hardware base-limit registers in Fig. 4.6, the two schemes are seen to be very close indeed. Fig. 4.7, which shows how the segment table is accessed will perhaps help to make this clear. Current implementations happen

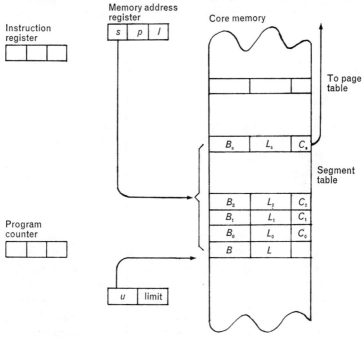

Execution sequence:
    Load memory address register from program counter
    Execute access cycle to fetch instruction into instruction register
    Load memory address register from instruction register
    Execute access cycle to
        set enabling flip-flops from C_s
        fetch operand
    Complete execution of instruction
    Increment program counter
    Repeat

Fig. 4.7

to be along the lines of Fig. 4.6 or Fig. 4.7 (although the access-class digits may be treated differently), but there is no reason why a simple virtual memory system, with no protection whatever, designed to work in conjunction with the protective system of Fig. 4.6, should not be a viable proposition.

The systems just described provide the programmer with all the facilities that he requires by way of protection, and it is likely that anyone setting out at the present time to design a computer would adopt one of them, or one of the many variants that suggest themselves. Further development of the scheme of Fig. 4.6 is, however, possible, and will be described in the next section.

Capabilities

The hardware systems so far discussed are designed to implement the first of the two approaches to the problem of protection that were distinguished above. Control is exercised through lists kept by the supervisor and consulted when applications for access to particular segments are made by user programs. The second method of control, namely by the issuing of tickets to authorised parties, will now be discussed.

The tickets are known as *capabilities* and, in order to obtain access to any segment, it is necessary for a process to have a capability for that segment. The term capability was introduced by Van Horn (1966); the idea was developed by Dennis and Van Horn (1966) who specified a set of *meta-instructions* that would be converted by an assembler or a compiler into supervisor calls. Using these meta-instructions, their system could be implemented on machines with protection systems similar to those that have just been described. In the system about to be explained, a special class of machine orders is provided which enables capabilities to be manipulated directly by the hardware. The idea of implementing capabilities in hardware is due to R. Fabry who, working under Professor Yngve at the Institute for Computer Research in the University of Chicago, made a study for a small-scale implementation (Fabry, 1968, 1971).

A capability comprises the name of a segment, or information about where it is in memory, and a statement of the class of access afforded. In fact, if we confine ourselves to a one-level memory only, then 'capability' is simply a new name for what we have called a segment descriptor. The base-limit registers (with the class digits included) are similarly renamed *capability registers*. The essence of the new scheme is that instructions which load a capability register from the memory, or unload a capability register into the memory, are treated as a separate class, and enabled and disabled separately from other instructions. The three access classes used in the scheme of Fig. 4.6 are extended as follows: (1) R, read data, (2) RW, read and write data, (3) RC, read capability, (4) RWC, read and write capability, (5) E, execute as program, (6) IO, input-output, and (7) EN, enter. An IO capability is needed in order to execute a program segment that contains input or output orders; the significance of an EN capability will be explained later.

Fig. 4.8 shows a processor designed to implement this system. It differs from Fig. 4.6 in that the base-limit register (now called a capability register) associated with the program counter now includes a *C* section, that extra enabling flip-flops have been introduced, and that the privileged mode flip-flop has been abolished. The enabling flip-flops are divided into two groups (A) and (B); during the execution sequence, the former are set from the *C* section of the selected operand capability register, and the latter from the *C* section of the capability register associated with the program counter. Although the privileged mode no longer exists, the trap feature remains. What exactly should happen when a trap occurs is discussed later. Capabilities are regarded as being objects of a different kind from other computer words; segments are either *data segments*, which contain data or program, or *capability segments* which contain a stock of capabilities. No segment contains both data words and capabilities.

In a programming system designed to go with the machine hardware that has just been described, a process would have a capability segment containing a stock of capabilities, and it might, in addition, have access to other capability segments. The only way in which it could get access to a segment of any kind would be first to load into one of the capability registers a capability for that segment. If the loaded capability were of class R (read data), for example, an instruction for loading one of the data registers could be executed, but one for copying a data register into memory would fail. If the capability were of class RC (read capability) then it would be possible to

73

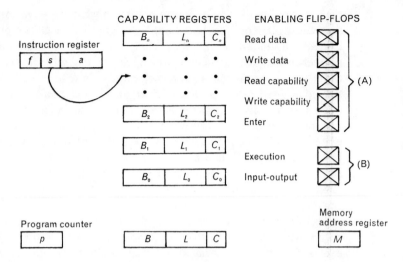

Instruction register

| f | s | a |

CAPABILITY REGISTERS

| B_n | L_n | C_n |

ENABLING FLIP-FLOPS

Read data
Write data
Read capability } (A)
Write capability
Enter

| B_2 | L_2 | C_2 |

| B_1 | L_1 | C_1 |

| B_0 | L_0 | C_0 |

Execution } (B)
Input-output

Program counter

| p |

| B | L | C |

Memory address register

| M |

Setting of enabling flip-flops

C_s	Read data	Write data	Read capability	Write capability	Enter
R	*				
RW	*	*			
RC			*		
RWC			*	*	
E					
IO					
EN					*

C	Exe-cution	Input-output
R	*	
RW	*	
RC		
RWC		
E	*	
IO	*	*
EN		

Execution sequence:
 Set $M = B + p$ if $p < L$; otherwise trap
 Fetch instruction
 Set enabling flip-flops (A) from C_s
 Set enabling flip-flops (B) from C
 Set $m = B_s + a$ if $a < L_s$; otherwise trap
 Execute instruction; trap if execution not enabled
 Increment p
 Repeat

Fig. 4.8

execute an instruction calling for the loading of a capability register, but not one calling for the loading of a data register. The fact that the capability loaded is either for a data segment or for a capability segment ensures that what is extracted from memory is either a data word or a capability, as the case may be; it would not be possible to copy a capability from a capability segment into a data register, since the capability for the capability segment would not permit the execution of a load data instruction. Thus, every routine would be able to do the things for which it had capabilities, but no others. No hard and fast distinction in the matter of privileges exists in this system between the supervisor and other programs. Some routines have a high degree of privilege on account of the capabilities that they possess, but they are otherwise indistinguishable from any other routine in the system.

The reader will perhaps understand from the above description how, when a process is established and working, the hardware constraints described above prevent capabilities and data getting mixed up; he will also understand that it is not possible for a process to generate in the arithmetic unit a capability for a segment to which it has no right and to plant it in a capability segment. He may, however, wonder how it is possible for a process to be created in the first place, or how a process can generate a further process. The answer is that there must be two systems routines, to which all processes have access, for creating data segments and capability segments respectively. The calling routine would supply the name to be given to the segment, and the creating routine would return with a capability for the new segment in one of the capability registers. The reason why the segment creating routines are able to break the rules is that they alone of all routines possess (in their capability segments) two capabilities for one and the same segment; one of the capabilities regards the segment as a data segment and the other as a capability segment. It is thus possible for such a routine to construct the capability using the arithmetic registers, put it in the special segment using the data capability, and then transfer it to a capability register using the other capability.

A problem of some importance concerns the calling of one routine by another. Two capabilities are necessary for starting a routine off properly, one for the routine itself, and another for its capability segment. If, however, the latter capability is made available to the

75

calling routine, a breach of protection may occur since it can well happen that the called routine has privileges which, in the interests of the security of the system as a whole, ought to be denied to the calling routine; for example, the called routine may have a capability for operating input or output equipment. The problem can be solved by providing a special machine instruction which will load a block of capability registers (two registers are sufficient) from the capability segment of the called routine, and then immediately send control to the routine itself, using one of the capabilities that has just been loaded. This instruction is known as an ENTER instruction, and will only work if an EN capability has been loaded into the appropriate capability register. An EN capability applies to the capability segment of the called routine, and a software convention requires that the first capability in this segment shall be a capability for the routine itself. The second capability should be for the capability segment of the routine. Return to the calling routine can be arranged through the agency of a return capability loaded in advance. If the programmer wishes to protect his own capability segment against malicious or accidental action by the called routine, then he must arrange that return is also by way of an ENTER instruction and an EN capability.

An operating system based on the principles that have just been described would thus consist of a collection of routines for such purposes as creating and destroying segments, servicing input and output devices including the multiplexer, together with compilers, assemblers, and loaders. Each of these routines would have access to a system capability segment and, in most cases, to one or more other capability segments as well. Presiding over the whole operation, and deserving as well as anything the name of 'supervisor', would be the co-ordinator (see p. 41). This would have capabilities for the various routines involved in establishing new processes and for all the user processes currently extant.

There is some room for debate as to what should happen when a trap occurs. Clearly, there should be a system trap routine which would deal with traps occurring in user programs and which were, from the point of view of those programs, fatal. Such a trap routine would, presumably, in the last resort, report to the scheduling algorithm and cause the program that had caused the trap to be aborted. However, it should also be possible for a user to write his own trap routine that would deal with those traps that he could foresee, and which would lend themselves to corrective action. If unable to deal with the situation, the user trap routine would call in the system trap routine. These requirements could be met if the hardware were so designed that, when a trap occurred, control were sent, by the equivalent of an ENTER instruction, to the beginning of the segment for which a capability existed in a specified capability register. The programmer would be responsible for placing in this register an EN capability for the system trap routine or one for his own specially written trap routine.

So far, all capabilities have been for segments physically loaded into core. It is possible to extend the idea to include capabilities for segments held in backing core, such as a disc or drum, or in a filing system. These are referred to as *pseudo-capabilities* by Yngve and Fabry. Arrangements must be made for generating the appropriate physical capability when a segment for which a pseudo-capability exists is loaded and (more difficult, for the reason given below) of destroying it or rendering it ineffective when the segment is unloaded. In a virtual memory system, the segment table may be regarded as a physical capability segment, containing capabilities for the currently existing page tables.

A problem arises when a capability is destroyed or converted into a pseudo-capability, since there may be many copies scattered through the various capability segments. It is possible, but time consuming, to make a scan of all capability segments in order to locate the copies in question. An alternative is to avoid the use of copies altogether and to use instead pointers to the original capability. This implies that chains of indirect references must be followed up and can also lead to loss of time. The problem is not trivial and no completely satisfactory solution has, to my knowledge, been proposed.

Some system is needed whereby a segment can be the guardian of a capability held in one of its capability segments without itself being able to make use of that capability. For example, it might be desired to confine the power of accessing a user's input buffer to a system input routine. Nevertheless, the logical place for the capability for that buffer to be stored would be in a capability segment belonging to the user's process. Means are required whereby the user's process itself could not make use of that capability which, however, it could hand on to be used by the input routine. There are considerable complications in handling this type of situation by means of ENTER instructions. It has been suggested that capabilities should have associated with them keys consisting of a small group of binary digits. A process would only be able to make use of a capability if it had the necessary match for the key. An alternative solution, more readily implementable, based on the use of chains of pointers has been described by Needham (1972).

If segments and files are regarded, as in MULTICS, as being the same things under different names, it will be seen that a comprehensive system, based on pseudo-capabilities, for handling segments throughout their lives as they move between the various levels of storage, from magnetic tape through discs and drums to core, will provide not only memory protection but will control the security of users' files as well. On this view, a user's file directory is simply an index to the capabilities that he may possess for segments (or files if he prefers that word) owned by him or by other users (*cf.* Dennis and Van Horn, 1966). No attempt, however, can be made here to follow up these interesting speculations any further.

General remarks

In the systems operating at the present time large parts of the supervisor run in privileged mode. In such systems the supervisor can be protected against object programs, and object programs can be protected against one another, but nothing can be protected against those parts of the supervisor that run in privileged mode. This is entirely satisfactory if the supervisor is fully debugged and if no hardware malfunctioning occurs. However, a system in which all processes, whether belonging to the supervisor or not, were allowed access (read-write, read only, or execute only, as the case might be) to those sections of the memory that concerned them and to no others, would enable the effect of a hardware failure or of a software error to be much better contained, since there would be a high probability that a violation of protection would occur before too much damage had been done to information held in memory. To be able to make corrections and changes to critical supervisor routines without running the risk of disastrous consequences if they did not work as expected would be particularly valuable to those charged with the maintenance of systems in operational use. It would similarly be valuable if a user could be enabled to protect one part of his program from other parts. Such a facility is, indeed, an essential requirement for the construction of systems within systems as described earlier in Chapter 3.

Provided that the simplest system for hardware memory protection exists—for example, a privileged mode and two or more base-limit registers—a protection system of arbitrary complexity can be implemented by software without the need to resort to purely interpretive working. With such simple hardware support, however, runtime overheads would set a limit on what was possible. The object of designing more elaborate systems of hardware support is to make it possible to implement a comprehensive system of protection that will not involve exorbitant runtime overheads. An additional motivation is the belief that in the last resort hardware protection gives greater security than purely software protection when system failure occurs.

The system used in MULTICS—and for which a substantial degree of hardware support is provided—is based on the concept of *rings of protection*. A process running in a given ring has access to material in rings outside that ring, but no direct access to material in inner rings. Any request for material in inner rings must be made *via* the supervisor which checks on the legitimacy of the request. This system represents a distinct advance on earlier systems and goes a long way to meet the requirements of the designers of systems and subsystems. For example, if some of the outer rings are not used by the supervisor, they can be put at the disposal of users who can then construct subsystems with their own internal protection. The system does not, however, meet all requirements. For example, it would not enable an input routine to be given access to an input buffer and an output routine to an output buffer, while simultaneously denying the input routine access to the output buffer and the output routine access to the input buffer. A hierarchic, or tree-like, system of protection would enable this particular requirement to be met, but the hierarchic form of organisation is not really suited to protection, and current research interest lies in systems that are non-hierarchic. The capability system that has been approached above from the hardware point of view is one of these. A capability system could be implemented on a conventional computer with a privileged mode of operation, but the frequent transitions to and from a privileged mode that would be necessary to administer the capabilities would present serious overheads. The Plessey System 250 (England, 1972) has a hardware capability organisation that closely resembles the one described in the previous section. The Cambridge CAP computer is an experimental computer in which the capability registers are loaded automatically on what can be described as the associative principle. The Cambridge CAP computer has no privileged mode, but does contain within the microprogram a significant section of microcode devoted to the manipulation of capabilities.

Designer's options

An attempt may be made to clarify the issues involved in memory protection by presenting a hypothetical decision tree that the designer of a computer might be imagined to traverse when deciding on a system of memory protection. Such a tree is shown in Fig. 4.9.

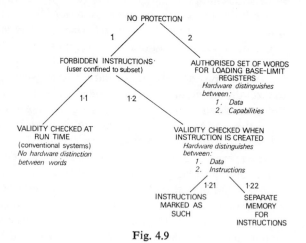

Fig. 4.9

A primitive computer has no mechanism whatever for memory protection. The provision of a base-limit register and the necessary mechanism for causing a trap to occur on violation is a step forward. This would, however, not afford any protection whatever if users were entirely free to load the base-limit register as they thought fit. The problem has, in fact, now become one of controlling what goes into the base-limit register. There are two alternative possibilities. One is to forbid the ordinary user to use instructions which load the register, that is to say to confine him to a subset of the total instruction set. This is shown in the decision tree as branch 1. The alternative (branch 2) is to allow instructions for loading the base-limit register to be freely used but to restrict what the ordinary user may put into it. An analogy from another field of security is provided by the alternatives of restricting access to a gun or of restricting access to the ammunition.

If the first branch of the tree is followed, it will be seen that there are two further alternatives. One is to check at runtime whether or not the instruction is permitted. This leads at once to the idea of the privileged mode and is, in fact, the system on which computers are conventionally designed at the present time. There is no restriction on an ordinary user writing one of the forbidden instructions in his program, but since he cannot operate in privileged mode a trap will occur when he attempts to execute it. The alternative (branch 1.2) is to check the validity of an instruction when it is created, that is when it first appears in binary form in a block of code. This method is not very practicable, but two conceivable ways of implementing it are shown in the decision tree. One is to have a special bit in each word that does not take part in accumulator operations, but serves to indicate whether the word is an instruction or a data word. The hardware will not execute as an instruction a word in which this bit is not on. A user could construct in the accumulator the binary form of an instruction, but he could only turn the indicating bit on by making use of a special instruction that would trap if the instruction so constructed were invalid. This also leads to the idea of a privileged mode in which the bit can be turned on whatever the instruction. An alternative (branch 1.22) is to have a separate memory for instructions instead of marking them by means of an indicating digit.

If branch 2 at the top of the tree is followed, it will be found to lead to the capability system that has been described in some detail. In this system, the hardware treats as entities of distinct type *data words* and *capabilities*. This is to be contrasted to the system described in the last paragraph in which the hardware treats as distinct entities *data words* and *instructions*. Conventional systems, of course, treat all words on the same footing whether they are instructions, data words, or pairs of numbers designed to go into base-limit registers. It is my personal view that systems in which the hardware distinguishes between data words and capabilities may have a future, but that any attempt to design a practical system in which the hardware makes a distinction between data words and instructions is likely to lead to a dead end.

5 Scheduling and Memory Allocation

With multi-programming, several object programs are resident in core at the same time, in addition to the permanently resident part of the supervisor. The object of multi-programming is to reduce the processor idle time that can otherwise occur when a single object program in core is waiting for a response (from the drum, a disc file, a magnetic-tape drive, or some other peripheral) and the supervisor is unable to make use of the time. Clearly this benefit is obtained only if there is enough core to accommodate the two or more object programs. If, for example, there are 32K words of core available for object programs, and 32K jobs are permitted, then it is doubtful, given an average mix of jobs, whether there will be enough short ones for the extra throughput achieved by multi-programming to justify the overheads incurred in providing it. These overheads manifest themselves in a larger supervisor and in more supervisor time. Thus, if jobs of maximum size are common, in order to make multi-programming pay off, one must buy a larger core memory—probably twice as large—as is necessary to hold the largest program permitted. This extra memory, together with the extra overheads of the supervisor, represents the price paid for the greater throughput.

In the above, it has been assumed that there is no paging. Paging enables better use to be made of core memory, so that less memory is required for a particular job. When this has been allowed for, however, the argument given above remains very much the same. More core is needed if several object programs are to be active at a given time than if only one is to be active.

In a system based on simple swapping, time slicing and core space allocation go hand in hand, since, when a program is resident in core, it is entitled to the use of the processor and only ceases to be so entitled when it is swapped out. In a multi-programmed system, on the other hand, the fact that a program is in core does not mean that it is necessarily entitled to the use of a processor. In fact, core space allocation and time slicing are separate yet related functions of the scheduling algorithm. Separate queues must be maintained for pro-

83

cesses that are both free to run and entitled to space in core, and for processes that are free to run but not so entitled. A process that becomes halted but will become free to run again in a short space of time does not necessarily lose its entitlement to core space. This is the case, for example, when a process is waiting for additional code or data to be loaded or for a peripheral buffer to become free. On the other hand, a process that becomes halted for a longer or an indeterminate time is likely to lose its entitlement to core space. This will happen, for example, to a process that is waiting for a console response or for an interrupt from a magnetic-tape deck.

Any implementer of a multi-programmed system has to arrive at a solution to the core space allocation problem. In the case of computers that have not been designed with time-sharing in mind—at the present time this means in practice computers that have no provision for hardware paging—the solutions inevitably have an *ad hoc* character. A description of their details, even if the necessary information were available, would serve little purpose, and certainly no coherent picture would emerge. Provided that there are adequate hardware relocation facilities, a program need not occupy the same area of core each time it is brought down from the drum, and programs can, if necessary, be moved around in core so as to consolidate into one continuous block scattered sections of available memory. In computers in which the hardware relocation facilities are less adequate, implementers tend to divide the memory into fixed partitions, and a given program is always brought down into its own partition. Clearly, this situation is far from ideal from the point of view of efficient utilisation of the whole memory.

Hardware paging, when first applied to time-sharing, was far from well understood and gave rise to a number of interesting and difficult problems. Some discussion of these will be given later. First, however, some remarks will be made about the life history of tasks in a time-sharing system, and the implications that this has on the space allocation and swapping problems. In this way an attempt will be made to bring out the principles that must underlie a successful system of core space allocation, irrespective of the hardware means by which it is implemented.

Taken as a whole, the tasks that are free to run will have differing expectations of life; some will run for brief periods before running to completion or being transferred to one of the queues of halted tasks, while others will run for long periods. The brief tasks will, however, be in the very great majority, and it is this fact that makes time sharing a worthwhile proceeding. In general, not enough is known in advance about an individual task to say how long it is likely to run. Experience has shown, however, that a task that has survived for more than a short period is likely to continue for some time and to merit special treatment. This may be expressed by saying that, subject to some limit, the expectation of life of a task increases with its age. This is unfortunate for the statisticians who find that, in order to make the mathematics tractable, they are often led to assume that distributions follow the Poisson law in which the expectation of life is independent of age. If this had been true in the CTSS, then there would have been no point in Corbató's scheduling algorithm described on p. 29.

Swapping and resident regimes

There will not be room in core for all the tasks that have been accepted by the co-ordinator and are free to run. It is convenient to refer to tasks that are regarded as being permanently resident in core in the sense that they will not be moved unless they become dead or dormant as being in the *resident regime*. Similarly, tasks that are subject to arbitrary removal, in order to make room for other tasks, are said to be in the *swapping regime*. Introduction of this nomenclature does not, in itself, imply a strategy of core management, since a task may be transferred from the resident regime to the swapping regime, or *vice versa*. It may, however, imply a policy in regard to the allocation of processor time, for example that fixed proportions should go to tasks in the two regimes. A practical strategy, which takes advantage of the non-Poissonian distribution of task life, is to regard all newly accepted tasks as being in the resident regime and if they survive to transfer them in due course to the swapping regime in the order in which they entered the resident regime. Provided that an adequate proportion of processor time is allocated to tasks in the resident regime, only a minority of them will ever enter the swapping regime, so that the overheads of swapping are not incurred for tasks that will only run for a very short time. When the system is running smoothly, it is intended that the queue of console-initiated tasks waiting to be reactivated should not be allowed to build up to more than a negligible extent. The number of jobs in the swapping regime that are actually in core at any moment is a parameter to be chosen, but there must be at least one such job.

A model based on these principles was described in detail in a paper presented at the Spring Joint Computer Conference in 1969 (Wilkes, 1969). Fig. 5.1 is taken from that paper. It is assumed that a separate core allocation system is provided for the supervisor. The argument in favour of doing this is that a good deal of information is available about the likely behaviour of supervisor processes that is not available in the case of object programs. Some supervisor routines, for example, are needed so frequently that they must be kept

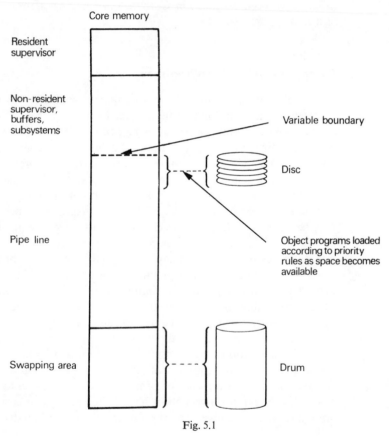

Fig. 5.1

permanently resident in core; on the other hand, it may be known that others, when they have finished running, will not be needed again for an appreciable time.

Tasks when first accepted by the scheduling algorithm enter an area of core known as the *pipeline* and are then in the resident regime. They work their way down the pipeline and, if they do not leave prematurely, eventually enter the swapping area and are then in the swapping regime.* A task may leave the pipeline if it reaches more than a temporary stoppage and it is then placed on the drum for reloading into the top of the pipeline when it becomes free. A task can also leave the pipeline if it runs to completion. A task may become halted without leaving the pipeline if it requires more memory space than has so far been allocated to it. Whenever a task leaves the pipeline tasks above it are moved down to fill the vacant space. This can result in space appearing at the top of the pipeline, in which case the scheduling algorithm can either load a new task at once or wait until additional space has become available. On the other hand, one of the other tasks in the pipeline, above the one that has disappeared, may be waiting for additional space; in this case, the space now available (or as much as is needed) is given to this task, any surplus being passed upwards for allocation to another waiting task or to be made available to the scheduling algorithm. One may think of a bubble of space passing upward and either being absorbed or partly absorbed on the way or reaching the top. The rate at which tasks are withdrawn from the pipeline and placed in the swapping region controls ultimately how much space becomes available for loading new tasks. In order that the system should operate in the manner contemplated, the rate of withdrawal must be high enough not only to create enough space for reactivated console tasks to enter the pipeline almost immediately, but also to allow an adequate quota of background tasks to be loaded.

The efficient operation of the system requires (1) that the average time taken for a task to pass through the pipeline should be much greater than the average life of a task, so that only a minority of tasks actually emerge from it, and (2) that the pipeline should contain

---

* It is to be clearly understood that references in the description of the model to tasks moving down the pipeline do not necessarily imply that in an implementation programs would be moved physically in core. A system in which a similar effect was obtained by software devices, or by paging hardware, would be a valid implementation of the model.

a sufficient number of tasks for there to be a high probability that at any instant there will be at least one task in core that is ready to run. There is no point in increasing the number of tasks in the pipeline beyond the point at which these conditions are met. What is important is the number of tasks in the pipeline not the total core space that they occupy. The amount of space needed in the pipeline will, therefore, vary from second to second according to the average size of the tasks. When there is space to spare, it is probably better to give it temporarily to the supervisor rather than to load redundant tasks. That is why the upper boundary of the pipeline is shown dotted in the figure.

A characteristic of the strategy that has just been described is that a console user who is making little demand upon the system by way of processor time—for example giving simple commands or making simple editing requests—receives a uniformly good response and is not conscious of changes in load. This is because none of the tasks that he creates survive long enough in the resident regime to pass into the swapping regime. Under conditions of heavy load, there will be more tasks in the swapping regime than under conditions of light load, and the user who creates long-lived tasks will find that he has to wait longer for his results to come back to him.

It is implicit in the above, that there is an upper limit to the amount of core space that may be occupied by any one program. This assumption is natural enough in the case of a conventional system, but ceases to be natural when a virtual memory is assumed. The lack of any firm knowledge of the amount of core space required by a program operating in a virtual memory environment is at the root of many of the troubles that have been experienced with paging algorithms, and the matter is taken up again on p. 91.

Paging

Paging as used in the Atlas computer was undoubtedly very successful; it may be that its success in that context led to its being applied to time sharing without a proper re-evaluation in the light of the new circumstances. The Atlas supervisor operated with multiprogramming and provided complete buffering for card readers, card punches, and similar input-output devices. At any one time, several programs shared the available core and, whenever the running program was held up waiting for a peripheral transfer, control was switched to another program. Paging was on a demand basis, no page being loaded until it was actually needed. A page loaded for a particular program would probably, but not necessarily, overwrite a page belonging to another program. Since there was no time sharing in the modern sense of serving a large number of on-line users, the number of active programs at any time was very small, and once a program had loaded the pages that it needed for a particular phase of its computation it could normally expect they would remain there; only pages that had not been used for some time would be in danger of being overwritten. Thus, it was intended that in normal operation there should not be a great deal of overwriting and subsequent reloading of pages. Multi-programming was seen as a way of avoiding idle processor time by overlapping input and output operations performed on behalf of one program with computation performed by another. In this context, input and output refers to punched cards, magnetic tape, and similar devices. The time spent in paging was relatively very small and in the original Atlas supervisor no attempt was made to overlap it; the processor was allowed to remain idle apart from some minor book-keeping tasks while a new page was being loaded and when this operation was complete running of the same program was resumed.

The conditions under which it was planned to run MULTICS were very different. In the first place, it was intended that there should be a large number of on-line users sharing the computer so that an individual program could expect, after a burst of activation, to lose all its pages and have to reload them when its turn came around once more. This extra paging corresponds, of course, to the operation of swapping. It was hoped that the paging time could all be overlapped by processor activity on programs free to run. Indeed, this was necessary in view of the greatly increased amount of paging as compared with the Atlas, and of the fact that some of this paging was to take place from a disc instead of a drum. The provision of segmentation as well as paging would inevitably encourage users to write programs that would involve more paging than the relatively simple ones run at an earlier period on the Atlas; this particularly applied to the writers of the supervisor which it was intended would, for the most part, operate under the same paging regime as would object programs.

Experience soon showed that while paging and segmentation might, in theory, be transparent to the program, the system writer at least should pay some regard to the way in which they would operate and plan his program strategy with a view to runtime efficiency; he should, for example, bind segments together in advance where possible instead of relying on runtime binding, and he should try to arrange that information needed for a particular purpose was, as far as possible, to be found on the same page or set of pages instead of being scattered over many pages.

In a typical system that is not based on the virtual memory concept there will, at any given time, be some processes loaded in core and others waiting for core but otherwise free to run. Whenever one of the running processes becomes halted, or exhausts its time slice, it is dumped and another process loaded. Each process in the system requires a known amount of core space, and no process is loaded until there is room for it. In a system with a virtual memory, what corresponds to loading a process is to bring one page into core and to authorise the process to demand other pages when it requires them. Experience with MULTICS has shown that it is advisable to arrange that all processes that are loaded in this sense are given processor time according to their seniority. Processor time is offered to the senior process in the first instance, and passed down to the next in order of seniority when that process comes up against a page wait. Processes low down in the hierarchy can only receive time by the process above them receiving time and coming to a page wait. As soon as a page has been loaded, the process that was waiting for it can pre-empt the processor if the running process is lower than itself in the hierarchy, but otherwise it must remain halted. It will be seen that the junior process is likely to receive time in short and infrequent bursts. Most probably, however, this will be all that it can use, since it is likely to be engaged in loading sufficient pages to enable it to run. Hopefully, by the time it has worked its way up the hierarchy, it will have loaded sufficient pages to enable it to absorb the greater part of the time that is offered to it.

The system will run smoothly only if pages loaded by a process tend to remain with it as it climbs up the hierarchy, and this requires that there shall be sufficient core space to meet the aggregated requirements of all the loaded programs. If there is a serious deficiency of core space, then pages will be overwritten by the demand paging mechanism almost as soon as they have been loaded. This is a situation known as *thrashing*. Its onset is sudden as the aggregated core space requirement of the loaded programs increases and it leads to a disastrous loss of performance. Allocation of processor time to loaded processes in order of seniority is an anti-thrashing measure, since it helps to control the competition between them for core space. It does not, however, offer a complete solution.

The working set

The principal difficulty lies in the fact that, in the paging systems so far described, there is no way of knowing how many pages a given process will need to load in order to be able to run with an acceptably small number of page waits. If this information were available, it would be possible to delay the loading of a process until it were known that sufficient pages could be made available in core to meet its needs without disturbing other processes. P. J. Denning took an important step towards rectifying this deficiency by introducing the concept of the *working set* which may be defined as follows: the working set is the set of pages that a process has accessed during a fixed interval of running time immediately preceding the instant at which it is measured (Denning, 1968, 1970). The working set is thus not only a function of time, but it also depends on the value chosen for the fixed interval. In practice, a suitable value must be arrived at by empirical means.

If it can be assumed that the size of the working set changes slowly with time, and if an estimate can be formed of this size, then it is clear that a powerful precaution against thrashing is to avoid loading a process unless it is known that there are enough pages available to accommodate the working set. Such an estimate can be formed by keeping a record of a suitable number of past page traps and analysing this record whenever a process loses its entitlement to core. Since processes vary a good deal in the size of their working sets, the number of processes loaded can be allowed to vary dynamically instead of being held at a fixed value low enough to be safe in all circumstances.

The resulting gain in efficiency will more than compensate for the administrative work involved in estimating the size of the working set. Since the working set can only be estimated from past experience, and since even this estimate is not available in the case of a new process, it will, on occasion, happen that thrashing sets in. If this can be detected, for example by noting that there is an increase in the frequency of page traps, then it is in principle possible to restore the situation by reducing the number of processes that are loaded.

Serious problems of stability are, however, involved, and the matter is discussed below in the section on the control of a paged operating system.

Once the size of the working set is accepted as an equivalent in virtual memory terms to the size of a program and provided that satisfactory means can be developed for estimating it, then any of the policies for core store management that have been advocated in non-paged situations can be taken over; for example the concepts of resident regime and swapping regime mentioned above can be assimilated.

Denning has drawn a distinction between *global* and *local* paging strategies. In the former all available page-frames are regarded as constituting a general pool to be drawn on by all loaded processes. In the latter each process is given its own quota of page-frames which it can reuse as it likes, but it cannot encroach on page-frames belonging to other processes. The advantage of a local paging policy is that one badly behaved process cannot interfere with the operation of the others; on the other hand, regarding page-frames as a resource to be drawn on by all processes may make it easier to achieve a high rate of utilization.

In the systems of demand paging so far considered no page is ever loaded until it is actually needed. It is natural to ask whether there would be any merit in loading the working set, or some approximation to it, as soon as a process is loaded; this is referred to as *pre-paging*. The advantage of asking for pages in bursts instead of singly is that a number of pages can then be picked off the drum during a single revolution and the aggregate latency time reduced. On the other hand some pages may be loaded and not used. Pre-paging cannot provide all the pages that are needed and must be combined with demand paging. It is desirable that pages that are demanded should be given priority on the drum channel. The current consensus of opinion appears to be in favour of pre-paging.

Page size

The choice of page size is clearly critical. Increasing the page size reduces paging overheads, both hardware and software, since fewer registers are needed in the associative memory and fewer entries in the page table; in addition paging traps are less frequent. On the other hand from the point of view of the efficient use of core space, a small page is desirable since the wastage due to pages not being full—referred to as core fragmentation—is reduced. The early systems all used a page size of 1K words. It might have been expected that any trend to use a smaller page size in order to reduce core fragmentation would be counteracted by the general trend towards large memories that is following on a falling of cost. However, it is noteworthy that the IBM System 370 uses a page size of 2K bytes.

One is apt to arrive at a different conclusion as to the optimum page size according to whether one looks at the matter from the point of view of the supervisor or from the point of view of an object program. The supervisor writer's interests are best met with a small page. Indeed, he would find it convenient to have available, in addition to regular pages, some extremely small pages of, say, 64 words, that could be used for input and output buffering and for similar purposes. The hardware of the GE 645 computer did, in fact, provide this facility, but it was found that any advantage in its use was nullified by the extra time spent in taking paging decisions.

Page migration

Usually in discussions of paging it is tacitly assumed that all pages are originally on a high-speed drum and that paging takes place between core memory and this drum. In fact, in a large time-sharing system there will inevitably be a variety of rotating storage devices and the great bulk of users' programs and data will necessarily reside on discs with relatively long access time. Paging to and from these discs takes much longer than paging to and from a high-speed drum, and if indulged in to any extent adds greatly to the problem of overlapping paging time by activity on other processes. One way in which this manifests itself is by increasing the total amount of core memory required.

It would hardly be feasible to adopt the obvious suggestion of copying everything relevant from the disc to the drum before beginning to page and, in any case, this procedure would defeat its own object by creating much extra traffic between the disc and the drum. The problem can be mitigated to some extent by arranging to keep pages belonging to the supervisor and other frequently used pages on the drum. Otherwise, however, it must be accepted that when first used pages belonging to users' programs will more often than not have to be fetched from the disc. Subsequently, they can be paged to and from the drum, although they are regarded as having their real home on the disc. From time to time, a cleaning-up operation is necessary to write back on to the disc pages that have been changed during the running of the program and to write up copies of new pages created by the program.

One approach to the page migration problem is to regard the memory system as having three levels and to treat the problem of writing back to the disc pages that are temporarily on the drum in a similar way to that of writing back to the drum pages that are temporarily in core. Similar procedures and similar methods of book-keeping can be used; the latter includes the use of bits to indicate whether a page has been referred to recently and whether its contents have been changed while it has been on the drum. Systems of this kind were put to practical trial both on MULTICS and on EMAS; EMAS even went so far as to introduce the concept of a drum working set. In both cases the conclusion arrived at was that the benefit obtained did not justify the overheads involved. It was found that a simpler system in which space on the drum was cleared periodically, or by a wholesale movement when congestion had set in, was more satisfactory. The problem has become eased by the use of discs with shorter latency times. A reference is made to the subject from the point of view of the filing system on p. 127.

Control of a paged operating system

An attempt will now be made to discuss in greater detail the problems that have been touched on in the preceding sections.

An operating system must maintain lists of processes that are in various stages of passage through the system. Three such lists may be identified as being essential; in practice these lists may be subdivided, but we need not here be concerned with the subdivisions. The *waiting process list* contains processes that have been presented to the system, but have not yet been accepted by the supervisor for the allocation of a share of processor time. The *accepted process list* contains processes that have been so accepted, while the *active process list*, or *loaded process list*, contains processes that are actually loaded, which in a paging system is taken to mean that they are entitled to have pages in core. The number of processes on the active list is called the *level of multiprogramming* and is denoted by L. L may have a constant value or it may vary dynamically.

The distribution of the available memory space between processes may be regarded as a problem in resource allocation. Since, however, core space is limited and must be reused, there is a corresponding problem in resource de-allocation. These two aspects, those of allocation and de-allocation, may be divorced from one another by maintaining a reserve of free page-frames which are not allocated to any process and are, therefore, available for allocation when required. The reserve of free page-frames is replenished by a routine— *the de-allocation routine*—that withdraws page-frames from processes, while the *allocation routine* is responsible for issuing page-frames to processes that require them. The special case in which the reserve is maintained at zero level is mentioned below.

Given the above framework of definitions, a system may be defined by specifying the following policies:

Scheduling policy
This is the policy according to which processes are transferred from the accepted list to the active list and *vice-versa*. It also covers the transfer of processes from the waiting list to the accepted list to make up for processes that have run to completion. The scheduling policy can be implemented by three separate routines, one for each of the three types of transfer just mentioned.

Process allocation policy
This governs the allocation of processor time to the processes on the active list, and is implemented by one routine.

Page allocation policy
This is implemented by the two routines that have already been mentioned, namely the allocation routine and the de-allocation

routine. To complete the specification of the paging policy, it is necessary to specify the circumstances in which the two routines are called in.

In a time-sharing system, it is to be expected that a process that has failed to run to completion, after being on the active list long enough to receive a certain quantum of processor time, will be transferred back to the accepted list to wait its turn for another period on the active list later. In a non-time-sharing system a process, once transferred to the active list, would stay there until it had run to completion.

Some of the factors that may be taken into account in deciding whether to transfer a process from the active list back to the accepted list are as follows:

(1) The amount of processor time that it has received while on the active list. Usually, on being transferred to the active list, a process is given an allocation of time that may depend, for example, on the total amount of processor time that it has already received and on the number of times that it has had a spell on the active list.

(2) Whether the process has reached an input/output wait (as distinct from a page wait) or is waiting for a semaphore.

(3) The current observed requirement of the process for page-frames (considered in relation to any estimate made when the process was transferred to the active list or to the aggregated requirements of other processes).

A process is removed from the system altogether when it runs to completion.

The decision to transfer a process from the waiting list to the accepted list may depend on the following factors:

(1) Whether the process is free to run; for example, whether any magnetic tapes needed have been mounted.

(2) The number of processes on the accepted list.

(3) The number of processes on the active list.

(4) The number of processes that have run to completion in the recent past.

(5) The priority (externally determined) attaching to the process.

A processor may become free as a result of the process on which it is working running to completion, being arbitrarily removed from the active list, or reaching a page wait. Depending on the policy adopted,

96

it may also become free if the running process has exhausted a slice of time allocated to it, without necessarily having consumed all its allocation of time for its current period of residence on the active list. When a processor becomes free, the following factors may be taken into account when deciding which process is to be given the use of the processor next:

(1) An arbitrary ordering of processes, for example, their positions on a round-robin.
(2) The relative seniority of the processes as determined by the order in which they entered the active list.
(3) The relative priorities of the processes.

Alternatively, the choice may be made on a random basis.

In the case of the allocation and de-allocation routines we have to consider when they are triggered, what action they take when triggered, and the criteria on which that action is based. The allocation routine can be triggered:

(1) When a new process enters the active list.
(2) When a process demands a page.

The action taken can be:

(1) To allocate a single page.
(2) To allocate a specified number of pages.

Factors taken into account in deciding whether the allocation can be met may be:

(1) Whether the process already has in core as many pages as it is allowed.
(2) The seniority of the process.
(3) The priority of the process.

The de-allocation routine can be triggered:

(1) When a process leaves the active list.
(2) When the reserve of free page-frames becomes zero or falls below a specified limit.
(3) At regular or quasi-regular intervals.

The action taken can be:

(1) To add a single page-frame to the reserve of free page-frames.

(2) To add a specified number of page-frames.

(3) To add to the reserve all page-frames satisfying certain criteria.

Factors taken into account in deciding whether a given page-frame shall be declared free may be as follows:

(1) Time, either real time or process time, that has elapsed since the page was last accessed.

(2) Whether the owning process is on the active list or not.

(3) Total number of pages already owned by the process.

(4) Seniority of owning process (absolute or in relation to those of other processes waiting for pages).

(5) Whether the page is owned by a single process or shared by several processes.

Nothing has been said about policy in relation to the size of the reserve of free page-frames, since this follows naturally from the policies that have been discussed above. If, for example, the de-allocation routine is triggered only when the reserve is exhausted, and if that routine delivers a single page, then in effect the reserve is maintained at zero level. Naturally, certain short cuts in implementation would be adopted if this were the case. One would probably have a single *placement routine* instead of separate allocation and de-allocation routines. The placement routine would have the responsibility both of deciding what page-frame to declare free and of issuing it to the demanding process.

A distinction may be drawn between policies in which a limit is set on the number of pages a process may own (not necessarily the same for all processes) and those in which no such limit is placed. This corresponds to the distinction made by Denning (1970) between local and global placement policies.

The above listings of factors to be taken into account are not intended to be by any means exhaustive. For example, in addition to the externally determined priority of a process, account may be taken of whether it belongs to a foreground or a background job and of its need for peripherals, such as magnetic tape drives.

The control of an operating system may be regarded as a problem in control engineering. The control engineer is concerned with such things as maximising throughput, minimising cost, and safeguarding the quality of the product; in general terms, he is concerned with the achieving of maximum efficiency, however that efficiency may be defined, Typically, if one attempts to push efficiency too far, one runs the risk of instability or of sudden loss of performance. The particular form of instability to which paging systems are subject is thrashing, which, as explained above, occurs when there is insufficient core space to meet the aggregated requirements of all the programs that are competing for it. To the extent that a computer system handling a stream of jobs can be regarded as analogous to a mechanical system or process plant, then the approach of the control engineer is relevant.

Control theory

The degree of complexity, or otherwise, that is necessary in a control system will depend on the degree of stability implicit in the basic design of the system to be controlled. If this is such that there is inherent negative feedback, then smooth operation may be possible without any superimposed control system. An example is provided by an electric motor which, if properly designed, will maintain a speed sufficiently constant for many applications without any form of control, drawing from the supply the amount of power required to meet the varying demands of a changing load. The simplest form of superimposed control is that summed up by the words *steam engine governor*. This type of control acts retrospectively on the occurrence of an error; it is, in fact, error-driven, and even in the steady state the error is never completely annihilated. A control system as simple as the steam engine governor will only work satisfactorily in an extremely small number of cases, another of which is the control of temperature by means of a thermostat. Watt, who invented the steam engine governor, was evidently lucky in that he had no problem over stability, and it was perhaps because this luck was not repeated that there was such a long interval before the modern subject of control engineering began to develop. As soon as control is applied to anything but the first derivative, or any delay is introduced, the problem of instability arises; one has only to imagine a steam engine governor that controlled the rate of flow of fuel to the boiler, or one in which a deliberate delay in the actuating of the steam valve were introduced, to appreciate this point. The theory of error-driven control systems in which the variables are continuous is now well understood.

99

In the case of systems in which a delay necessarily occurs between an action becoming necessary and the decision to take it becoming effective, a control system that can look ahead is required. If the delay is small and the variables are continuous, the look ahead can be based on the current rate of change; the widely used P.I.D. (proportional, integral, derivative) controllers work on this principle. If, however, the delay is more serious, such methods are not sufficient to achieve stability and some knowledge of plant dynamics must be built into the control system. This is where a model of plant operation or of product behaviour comes in. The control system consults the model before deciding on the action to be taken in the plant. An essential feature is that the model should operate more quickly than the plant. In some cases, hill-climbing techniques can be used; that is, alternative courses of action can be tried on the model and the best one selected. Models typically contain parameters whose values must be continuously estimated with the aid of data obtained from the plant; a case in point is a parameter describing the efficiency of a catalyst in a reaction vessel. If, however, one does not wish to be concerned with the details of a model, one can think of it as a black box into which a number of inputs are fed and from which come one or more outputs that are used by the control system to decide on action. The fact that the model has to determine its own parameters means that the outputs are functions of past values of the inputs as well as of current values and may, therefore, be biased towards the past.

In some cases, *open loop control*, based on a model, may be entirely satisfactory in itself. In this case the outputs of the model are used to control the system without any feed back. On the other hand, it may be necessary to supplement open loop control by an additional superimposed control loop of the steam engine governor type.

Often it is necessary to add *safety devices* that come into action when the control system fails. These may be divided into two classes: those which enable operations to continue and those which shut the plant down altogether. An example of the first class is the safety valve on a boiler and of the second the emergency control rods in a nuclear reactor. In many cases, the former class are not correctly to be regarded as safety devices at all, but as an additional level to the control system. Their presence may enable the next lowest level of control to be simplified and designed in a less conservative manner, with a resulting improvement in average efficiency. Although blowing off steam is inefficient, the presence of the safety valve enables a boiler to be run nearer to its maximum safe working pressure than would otherwise be the case.

Flow of processes

Fig. 5.2 shows in diagrammatic form the way in which processes flow through the system. The flow of processes between the accepted list and the active list is controlled by two 'valves', V_2, V_3, and the flow of processes from the waiting list to the accepted list is controlled by the 'valve' V_1. A number of processes of varying shapes and sizes are shown as being currently on the accepted list with pages attached to them. Pages are withdrawn to the reserve through the 'valve' V_5 and supplied to the processes as required through the 'valve' V_4. The processor—only one is shown in the diagram for simplicity—can be associated with any process on the active list through the 'switch' S_1. It is to be emphasised that the figure is entirely diagrammatic and that the analogy with a process plant is not to be taken too seriously. $V_1, V_2, \ldots, V_5$ and S_1, may be referred to as *control points*.

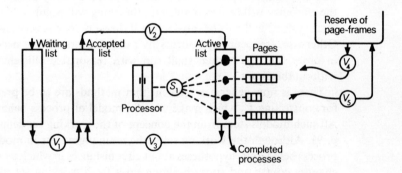

Fig. 5.2 The flow of processes through a time-sharing system.

V_3 is controlled by one of the routines implementing the scheduling policy, S_1 by the processor allocation routine, and V_4 and V_5 by the allocation and de-allocation routines. Some of the considerations on which the policies behind these routines are based have already been given. In all cases the necessary decisions can be taken on the basis of information available at the time without any need to look into the future. In choosing the policies an attempt should be made to give the system the highest possible degree of intrinsic stability in the sense that an electric motor has intrinsic stability. Some policies would obviously do just the contrary; an example is a de-allocation policy that would cause the most recently used page-frame, rather than the least recently used one, to be declared free. It is not, however, always easy to see what the effect of a particular policy will be as regards intrinsic stability (see, for example, Alderson *et al.*, 1971).

In a process plant, a control engineer would install at points such as V_3, V_4, V_5, S_1, controllers taking account of present values. Control of V_2, however, is not such a simple matter. If too few processes are allowed to enter the active list, there will be processor idle time and consequent inefficiency. On the other hand, if the number of processes on the active list is allowed to increase beyond a certain point, there will be insufficient pages to satisfy their needs and thrashing will occur. If processes were uniform in their paging requirements, the routine for controlling V_2 could be designed to keep the number of processes on the active list to a predetermined number. Indeed, some systems do work in this way. The number is chosen conservatively, in the hope that, with the workload actually encountered, the efficiency will be acceptable and thrashing will occur only rarely. Such systems will only be satisfactory if the work load is very uniform. Otherwise, frequent adjustments by the operators will be necessary in order that the system shall run with reasonable efficiency and without thrashing.

There is now general agreement that methods are to be preferred for controlling V_2 which make use of a model of process behaviour. All such models stem from the concept of the working set defined on p. 91. Although the working set is the main ingredient in models of process behaviour, hypotheses about circumstances in which a process changes course and starts building up a fresh working set may be incorporated, as may also means of estimating the working set of a process that has not yet run. For example, regard may be had to the language in which the program is written, to the number of statements it contains, to its provenance, and so on. It would be nice to have a model that was capable of more accurate prediction and relied less heavily on observations from the past. It is not easy, however, to discern any principles on which such a model could be constructed.

Since the model used is not perfect, thrashing will sometimes occur and another level of control of the safety valve type is, therefore, necessary. This could be provided by arranging to detect the onset of thrashing—by an increase in processor idle time or in the rate of paging—and to take suitable action to restore stability. Some provision for human decision is necessary at this point, if only to purge from the system jobs whose working sets are too large for them to be effectively run.

In one respect Fig. 5.2 is misleading in that it may make the reader think of a process plant working with continuous fluids. In fact, in a computer system we are concerned with discreet jobs or tasks, and the numbers involved at the critical points are small. Moreover, there is nothing corresponding to the inertia of fluid flowing in a pipe. Thus it is not possible to take over from control engineering any of the theory that applies to error-driven control systems operating with continuous variables and in which use is made of derivatives for stabilisation. I regard as ill-conceived attempts that have been made to design paging systems that always tend to move towards a condition of thrashing, and as this condition becomes detected to back off. A system that continually loads one process too many, detects the onset of thrashing, and corrects the condition by unloading one of the processes will inevitably spend a significant amount of its time thrashing or recovering from thrashing. The object is to prevent the system from thrashing and once thrashing has started the damage has been done.

There is not much that needs to be said about the control of V_1. It is desirable that the accepted list should always contain a good mix of jobs as regards the demands they make on the various system resources. Apart from this it is sufficient to keep the number of processes on the accepted list topped up to a suitable value that is not very critical. If too many processes are allowed on to the accepted list the result will be a poor response.

Queueing theory

The approach made in this chapter is complementary to the more usual statistical approach by way of queueing theory. Statistics, being concerned with an average over all possible situations, can throw no light on the way a system will behave in particular circumstances. Also it does not form a good basis for a discussion of stability. On the other hand, statistical considerations should be highly relevant to the discussion of such questions as how much channel capacity, buffer space, etc., must be provided in order to secure efficient operation without congestion. The difficulty is that there is no way of deciding in advance what values to give to the fundamental statistical parameters describing task life, users' response, etc. It is perhaps partly for this reason that rather disappointing practical gains have come from the large amount of effort that has been devoted to statistical studies of paging systems.

Examples

The table shows how a number of paging policies that have been implemented or suggested may be described in the foregoing terms. Each row of the table refers to a particular combination of policies and the last column indicates, where appropriate, a system that has been implemented or discussed in the literature that comes near to the one of which an outline is given in the preceding columns. The system outlined in the first line of the table uses simple demand paging with a global paging algorithm according to which the page longest in core is always overwritten, irrespective of the process to which it belongs. There is no time-sharing and a process reaching an input or output wait is not removed from the active list, although it may, in the course of time, lose most or all of its pages. The second line shows a similar system with time-sharing. In both these systems processes on the active list are arranged in a round-robin and whenever a process reaches a page wait the processor is offered to the process next in cyclic order. The disadvantage of this strategy is that control tends to pass to the process that has been waiting longest and hence is most likely to have lost some of its pages. It would be better to offer the processor, whenever the current process reaches a page wait, to one of the other processes chosen at random. This in fact, is what the strategy degenerates into under conditions of heavy paging when, at any given time, only one or two of the processes will be free to run. A disadvantage of these types of strategy is that the processes

104

compete with each other for pages on more or less equal terms and the consequence will, as like as not, be a disorderly scramble.

This defect is corrected in the system used in MULTICS (see line 3 of the table) and already described on p. 90. Some order is introduced into the competition for pages by assigning the processor always to the most senior process that is free to run. The seniority of a process is determined by the order in which it entered the active list. We have here a good example of the way in which the intrinsic stability of a system can be promoted by good choice of an algorithm. In MULTICS a form of prediction based on the working set model is used to control V_2. The actual algorithms used in MULTICS are complex and information about them will be found in Organick (1972). Line 4 shows a non-time-sharing system of interest in that it provides implicit control of the level of multi-programming. Processes are arranged in order, although the order is determined by an externally assigned priority rather than by seniority of loading. In Wharton's system (Alderson *et al.*, 1971) on which this line of the table is based, the priority applies not only to the allocation of the processor, but also to the delivery of pages from the drum. If, when a processor demands a page, the reserve is empty, a page frame is commandeered from a process junior to the demanding process, the process chosen for raiding being the most junior one that has pages in core. If the demanding process is itself the most junior process, or if all the processes junior to it have no pages in core, then the demanding process is halted. There may thus be a number of processes on the active list that have no pages in core and have no prospect of becoming free to run until a senior process runs to completion and releases page frames to the reserve. The effective level of multi-programming is given by the number of processes that have pages in core rather than by the number on the active list and varies dynamically. The system has the property that the highest priority process runs in effect as though it were alone in the computer; there is no reason why it should not go on demanding pages until it occupies all the page-frames in core and no other process is able to run. In some situations this may be just what is desired; in others, it would be regarded as a disadvantage that the senior process never loses pages, even those it has not touched for some time. In a modification of the system, pages that have not been touched for a certain length of time are periodically returned to the reserve.

	V_2 LOADING OF A NEW PROCESS	S_1 ALLOCATION OF PROCESSOR	V_3 UNLOADING OF A PROCESS	V_4 PAGE FRAME ALLOCATION	V_5 PAGE FRAME DE-ALLOCATION	NOTES[1]
1	keep L constant	round-robin; a process loses processor on reaching an I/O wait	never	on demand	zero reserve; take LRU[2]	cf. Atlas[3]
2	ditto	round-robin; a process loses processor on reaching a page wait	on reaching an I/O wait; on exhausting time allocation	ditto	ditto	time-sharing with demand paging
3	keep sum of working sets less than core capacity	Senior process free to run pre-empts processor	on reaching an I/O wait; on exhausting time allocation	by pre-paging; on demand	on completion; on unloading; if reserve empty take LRU[2]	cf. MULTICS[4]
4	keep L constant	highest priority process free to run pre-empts processor	never	on demand	on completion; if reserve empty take LRU from process of lowest priority that owns pages	cf Wharton[5]
5	load if space allocation (based on working set) is less than reserve	round-robin; a process loses processor on reaching a page wait	on reaching an I/O wait; on exhausting time allocation; on exceeding space allocation	by pre-paging; on demand	on completion; on unloading; at intervals take pages not in current working set of any process.	cf. EMAS (Whitfield[6])

[1] Systems mentioned in this column resemble in some, if not all, of their features the one outlined in the earlier columns.

[2] Least recently used page irrespective of owning process.

[3] See Kilburn et al. (1962).

[4] See Organick (1972).

[5] See Alderson et al. (1971).

[6] See Whitfield and Wight (1973).

Line 5 refers to a paging system based on a through-going use of the working set model that has been implemented for EMAS, a system developed on an ICL (English Electric) 4–75 computer by a team led by H. Whitfield at Edinburgh University. It is of interest in that it uses a local, as distinct from a global, paging policy. A process, on being transferred to the active list, is given a *core allocation* and a *time allocation*. In the case of a process that has not yet run, these are determined by arbitrary rules. Periodically the working set of each process on the active list is re-computed and page-frames containing pages no longer in the working set are added to the reserve. If, in spite of this, the process tries to exceed its core allocation, it is immediately returned to the accepted list: It is similarly returned if it exhausts its time allocation or if it reaches a console wait. When a process is so removed, its working set is re-computed and both its core allocation and its time allocation are reassessed. The reassessment is based on the original assessment and on the reason for removal. A process that has run out of time, but whose working set is within its core allocation, will perhaps next time be allowed more time but less core. When it is returned to the active list, its working set will be pre-paged. Similarly, a process that has run out of space will have its core allocation increased. However, the fact that it has run out of core is taken as an indication that quite possibly it has moved to another part of its virtual memory, so that its former working set is no guide to the number of pages that it will require in future. No pre-paging is done, therefore, when such a process is re-activated, and it must load its pages one by one on a demand basis. The core allocation, rather than the size of the working set itself, is used to control V_2; no process is transferred to the active list unless there is enough space in the reserve to meet its maximum authorised requirement as specified by its core space allocation, a suitable allowance being made for shared pages. The level of multiprogramming is thus determined dynamically. A consequence of the use of a local paging policy is that each process is able to operate within the number of page-frames allocated to it, and the misbehaving of one process cannot affect other processes.

6   Satellite Computers and Computer Networks

So far this book has been concerned with systems containing either a single processor or a number of processors each capable of accessing a common memory bank. A criss-cross switch connecting the processors and the memory modules is an essential component of such a system. The cost of the switch and the fact that it degrades memory performance (seriously if very fast memories are used) are important considerations. For some purposes, processors complete with their own memory are more appropriate; a number of these may be linked together, or may be connected as satellites to a multi-processor system. In either case, what results is a *multi-computer system*.

Self-contained computers may be connected as satellites to a time sharing system in a number of ways and with a number of different objects in view. In some cases, it may be desired to have self-contained computing power at a distance from the main system, and connected to it only intermittently or through a channel of narrow bandwidth. This is economical if the small local computer can handle the greater part of the work and it makes unnecessary the long-distance transmission of large quantities of data. Satellite computers that are specially adapted to particular problems also have their place in a comprehensive system. One such type of satellite, of which we shall no doubt hear much in the future, is a computer specially designed for handling long numerical calculations that involve little or no interaction with discs or drums, but which call for computing speed of the highest order obtainable. Indeed, it is hard to see how, in view of the degradation of memory performance by the criss-cross switch referred to above, really super-speed memories can be properly used unless they are associated directly with a processor. Another specialised satellite is one used to control a cathode-ray tube display.

Satellite computers on a time-sharing system

There are many ways in which the satellite may be connected to a

108

time-sharing system. One way is *via* the multiplexer as though it were a teletype, or a VDU. This has the advantage that no changes or special arrangements in the time-sharing system are needed in order to accommodate the satellite. Account must, however, be taken of the fact that the response of the time-sharing system to messages sent to it is not always easily predictable, especially if some of the programs being used, either in the satellite or in the main system, are not fully debugged. It is, therefore, to be preferred that messages from the supervisor of the time-sharing system should be passed to a human being rather than to a machine. This kind of problem arises whenever two automatic interactive devices are connected together. A case in point is the unhelpful consequences that ensue when an automatic telephone calling device is met by an automatic answering device.

One method of dealing with the problem in the case of a satellite computer is to arrange that all messages from the supervisor should be routed to the console attached to the satellite. More often than not the user will have two programs working for him, one in the satellite and one in the main system. It should be possible for him to use his console to send a message either to his program in the satellite or to the main system.

It will be seen that, in addition to its other functions, the satellite computer acts as a message-switching device. In order that messages may be sent to the right places, it is necessary that some, or all of them, should be preceded by a tag indicating their correct destination. Since the designer of the satellite system presumably has no control over the main time-sharing system, it is best to assume that messages from the supervisor are untagged. Such messages are routed to the user's console. The user can, however, write any program that he proposes to run in the main system so that messages from it are tagged according to their destination; untagged messages would go to the user's console and tagged messages to his program in the satellite. There is more freedom with regard to the tagging of messages typed by the user on his console. A convenient arrangement might be for tagged messages (with the tag removed) to be directed to the main system and untagged messages to the user's program in the satellite.

To implement a system of the type described, one would start by fitting up the satellite with a fully buffered input-output system of the type common in time-sharing systems (see p. 26). The line to the main system would be treated very much as a line to a console. It would have an input buffer, which would be examined at frequent intervals to detect the arrival of a character, and it would have an output buffer. The scanning could be avoided by the provision of a special hardware interface to the line, which would send an interrupt signal to the satellite whenever a character arrived. The routines associated with the line and with the user's console would be responsible for routing messages according to their tags. At suitable intervals, a clock interrupt would cause control to be sent to a display routine which would initiate the display of the picture defined by the current display table (see p. 115).

The system would be operated in the following manner. It is assumed that the programmer has written for the two computers a pair of co-operating programs appropriate to his particular problem and that the program that is to be run in the large system has been filed away on the disc. The user then loads his program into the satellite and sends control to it. At this stage, it may only be running in an idling loop. Working from the console on the satellite, he then logs in to the main system, loads his program in that system and activates it. He is then in a position to go ahead.

A more elaborate way of connecting a satellite to a time-sharing system will now be described. This type of connection is very powerful, and enables the user to exploit rather fully the facilities of both computers. The message-handling problem is avoided by providing the user with a console on the main system in addition to the console on the satellite. He uses the former for logging in and for any direct communication with the main system that may be necessary.

The main system and the satellite are connected by a data link capable of passing data in either direction. There is also a pair of interrupt channels, one of which is used by the main system to send an interrupt signal to the satellite. and one by the satellite to send an interrupt signal to the main system. In other words, either computer is able to interrupt the other. The main system can expect an immediate response from the satellite, but may itself take some time to reply to a message from the satellite. It is possible to arrange that both data and interrupt signals should be sent along the same physical channel; this is almost essential if the satellite and main computer are separated by more than a small distance.

The small computer needs a supervisor and I shall refer to this as the *executive* in order to avoid confusion with the supervisor in the main system. The executive may be simple or complex depending on the facilities required and on the amount of core memory available in the satellite. A minimal set of facilities that might be provided by the executive are as follows:

(1) To accept from the supervisor an address in the memory of the satellite to which a block of binary information later to be sent along the data link is to go.
(2) To accept the block of information and put it in the specified place.
(3) To accept from the supervisor an address in the memory of the satellite and send control to that address.

If the supervisor had occasion to send a block of data over to the satellite, then it would, on completion of the operation, send control back to the executive. If, on the other hand, the block of information sent over were a program, it would send control to the beginning of that program. If data in the satellite has to be sent to the large machine, the supervisor first sends over a program which will, when executed, cause the required transfer to take place. It then sends control to that program, and, when the program has finished, control reverts to the executive.

We have here a situation in which the supervisor may be said to be in over-all charge of everything that goes on; the satellite is allowed as it were, no life of its own. If a program has to be executed in the satellite, that program is first prepared in the large computer, and then sent over in binary form ready for running. All the software necessary for running programs in the satellite—compilers, assemblers, loaders, etc.—are, in fact, to be found in the main computer. The supervisor keeps a storage map for the satellite, so that information is constantly available to it about everything that is in the memory of the satellite and where it is located.

User-support system

An important use of a satellite computer in a time-sharing system is for handling communication between the users and the system. A computer used in this way is often referred to as a *front-end* computer.

In its simplest form a front-end computer simply functions as a multiplexer, but it may also handle local line editing and provide for the connection of remote batch terminals to the system. I propose in this section to examine the advantages of splitting the functions of the operating system between the main computer and the front-end computer.

A time-sharing system of the type with which this book is concerned performs two distinct functions. One of these is to provide support to the user in his capacity as a user of the system, irrespective of the particular application on which he is working. This includes facilities for filing programs and data, editing files, and handling their administration with the aid of a file directory. It may also include the provision of interactive services of a type that a user is likely to require from time to time, such as a JOSS-like system for doing small calculations. The second function of a time-sharing system is to put what may be described as brute computing power at the disposal of a user when he needs it. This implies the availability among other things of a powerful processor.

So far it has been assumed that both kinds of facility can, and normally should, be provided by the same computer system, possibly a multiprocessor system. The former facilities can, however, be provided by a front-end computer which, together with its software, may then be described as a *user-support system.*

A user-support system consists of a processor to which terminals of various kinds, including teletypes, are connected, together with data links from other computers; it is itself connected as a satellite to the main computer system in the manner described in the latter part of the preceding section. Disc stores (extensible as required) for holding users' files are connected so as to be directly accessible both to the user-support processor and to the main system. The executive that runs within the user-support processor is responsible for the administration of the filing system including the maintenance of the file directories, the control of access, and the dumping of files on to magnetic tape for integrity and archival purposes. The user-support system enables a user to create and edit files and to prepare a job for insertion into the job stream of the main computer. The main computer must have an operating system capable of accepting jobs with differing priorities attached to them and running them, preferably on a time-shared basis, so that a long job does not block the entire system. It makes direct access as required to the files on the disc and either returns the results to the user-support system or puts them into specified files. Any large special purpose data bases (see p. 146) would be attached to the main computer rather than to the user-support system. The amount of software required to support the facilities just described is not small and, since any other interactive services (such as a JOSS-like system) that are required must also be provided as part of the user-support system, it is necessary that the satellite computer in which it runs should have a generous amount of core memory; in fact, together with its peripherals, it is by no means a small computer.

A division of function in this way has obvious advantages at the present time when completely integrated systems must even now be regarded as still in the experimental stage, but when most large computers are provided with operating systems that meet the above requirements. However, there are also advantages to be seen on a longer term. The use of a separate user-support system would enable a change to be made in the main computer without the users having to adapt themselves to an entirely new mode of operation. They would have to learn the job description language for the new computer and become familiar with the compilers and other facilities provided by it, but they would retain for use in the new context the filing and editing systems that were familiar to them. It would be possible for a user-support system to feed two or more main computers, and there is no reason why these computers should not be of different type and manufacture. A user-support system, once the users had become accustomed to it, might continue to meet their requirements over a long period of time, especially if the filing capacity could be expanded more or less indefinitely. A new user-support system could, however, be brought into operation without seriously interrupting the flow of work through the main computer or computers.

Displays in a time-sharing environment

Video display units (VDUs) have already been discussed in Chapter 1. Some of these provide facilities for drawing lines and arcs and meet many of the requirements of computer graphics. They do not, however, permit the user to work interactively with a display. For this purpose the display must be directly connected to a computer, which may be either free-standing or may be a satellite on a larger system.

The essential component of a digital display is a cathode-ray tube whose x and y plates are connected to the outputs of a pair of digital to analogue converters which can be fed with numbers from the computer; it must be possible for the spot to be switched on and off under computer control. The most direct way for an operator to interact with the display is by means of a light-pen. In its simplest form, this consists of a small photocell on the end of a rod. If the light-pen is placed on the glass surface of the cathode-ray tube screen, and if the spot passes underneath it, the photocell emits a pulse. The photocell output is connected either to an interrupt input of the computer or to a flip-flop whose state can be sensed and reset by the program. In either case, the program can be written to take account of the fact that the light-pen has seen the spot.

From the user's point of view, the light-pen serves two distinct purposes. In the first place, it can be used to draw. For this purpose there must be a tracking program which causes a small cross— known as a *tracking cross*—to be displayed on the screen. When the light-pen is pointed at the centre of the cross, there exists a symmetrical situation which is recognised as such by the tracking program, and the tracking cross remains at rest. If the pen is moved slightly, then the tracking program takes the necessary action to re-centre the cross. The effect is that the tracking cross follows the pen across the screen. The operator may also use the light-pen to point at some object being displayed on the screen, and to indicate that he is about to give instructions relating to it. The light-pen sees the pulse of light and causes the program to be interrupted when the object in question is being traced out. The program thus receives an unambiguous indication of which object is being pointed at.

There are other ways of interacting with a display. One is the obvious way of typing on a keyboard messages which the computer interprets as instructions relating to the display. A more direct competitor with the light-pen is a joystick that can be moved in two dimensions and controls a spot on the screen independently of the main display. A joystick has the disadvantage that one cannot easily write or draw with it. A better device is one invented at the Rand Corporation and known as the Rand tablet (Davis and Ellis, 1965).

This has a flat writing surface under which are two orthogonal sets of parallel conductors spaced very close together. These conductors are fed with pulses which give the x and y co-ordinates of any point on the tablet in binary form—in fact, in Gray code. A metallic pen placed on the tablet will then pick up, by capacity coupling, pulses which represent the co-ordinates of the point at which it is placed. These pulses are fed into the computer and cause a spot to be displayed. The operator must get used to the fact that when he writes on a Rand tablet the writing does not appear under the pen but on the screen, Other tablets equivalent from the point of view of the user to a Rand tablet, but working on a variety of different principles, are now available.

Unless some additional hardware is provided, however, a tablet—or, for that matter, a joystick—is not very good for pointing, since every time the spot is displayed in the course of tracing out a picture a test must be made to see whether it is being displayed at a point whose co-ordinates are being pointed at. This is effective, but time-consuming. In order to make the tablet equivalent to the light-pen as far as pointing is concerned, it is necessary to provide two extra registers which always hold the co-ordinates of the pen and two sets of coincidence circuits linking these registers to the x and y registers of the display. It is, incidentally, better not to associate these extra registers permanently with the tablet, but to make them available to the programmer so that he can put anything there he likes. Most often, of course, he will put the co-ordinates of the pen.

Extra hardware of the kind just mentioned can pay good dividends if it enables the display to be speeded up and the complexity of what can be displayed without flicker increased. Another example is the provision of circuits for automatic edge detection which will interrupt the computer whenever the spot reaches the edge of the screen.

Many displays associated with small computers run independently of the computer itself. The programmer constructs in the memory a *display table* which contains, in effect, instructions to the display for moving the spot. Once the display is started it runs autonomously through the display table while the computer is doing something else, the display stealing memory cycles as it requires them. A paramount consideration in the design of a display system is that information should be efficiently packed in the display table. This is a matter for the hardware designer primarily, although, of course, the

115

programmer is expected to make the best use that he can of the facilities with which he is provided. In some systems analogue circuits are provided for drawing lines or arcs between digitally defined points.

The difficulty about operating a display on a time-sharing system is that each user of such a system receives service only intermittently. A user with a display, however, requires that the display should be animated continuously. He also requires instantaneous response to any actions he may make with the light-pen, whether he uses it for drawing or for pointing. Again, if he is displaying a three-dimensional object, he may wish to be able to make it rotate by manipulating a joy-stick and thus obtain a three-dimensional effect. The necessary instantaneous response to these and similar actions can best be obtained if the display is driven by a computer connected as a satellite on the time-sharing system. Except where very simple applications are concerned, the computer driving the display must have sufficient core memory to hold the data structure representing the object being displayed as well as the necessary programs. Early attempts were made to work with satellite computers that were not large enough for this, so that the data structure had to be kept in the main computer. The operator would queue requests for modifications to be made to the material displayed and these requests would be serviced at irregular intervals by the time-sharing system. These methods were not very successful and they have fortunately been rendered unnecessary by the increase that has taken place in the power of low-cost computers. In computer-aided design, and in other applications needing a high degree of interaction, the satellite computer controlling the display is no longer likely to be a small one.

Computer networks

The term *computer network* will be used in this book to describe systems in which separate computers on remote sites are interconnected. It is usual to distinguish two types of computer network. There are *homogeneous networks* in which the various computers comprising the system are compatible in the sense of having similar instruction sets and the same word length; more likely than not they will be of the same manufacture. The object of providing the interconnection is so that there may be facilities for load-sharing and mutual support in case of breakdown. These facilities are invoked by the operating staff as and when required. The system may or may not include a number of small computers used for switching or interface purposes. Although a large number of homogeneous computer networks have come into existence to meet specific needs, the software problems involved do not appear to have been discussed or even formulated in general terms.

The term *heterogeneous network* is used in reference to the interconnection of a number of separate computer systems, each of which is a self-contained entity designed to serve a particular community. Such systems have their own standards and operating conventions, and are likely to differ widely, reflecting as they do the differing philosophies of their designers. In spite of these differences, communication between different systems is entirely possible. We have always had a system of effecting communication between widely differing organisations, namely the use of alphabetic characters. It is only recently, however, that the use of filing systems has led to the storage within computers of information in character form. Not only can such information be used directly by human beings, but it can also be absorbed into other computer systems. Once in a computer, of course, information can be transformed by algorithm to any form in which it is required. A generalisation of the alphabetic character is the byte, and this form is indicated for the transmission of large quantities of data which do not have to be handled by human beings.

In the absence at the present time of a digital communication network, the telephone system has come into extensive use for data transmission. It is necessary for the digital information to be modulated on to a carrier at the sending end and to be demodulated at the receiving end; the device that fulfils these functions is known as a *modem* or *data set*. While the use of the telephone system for data transmission can undoubtedly be developed further, the real need is for a separate purely digital network. This would be based on a number of strategically sited digital exchanges connected together by high-speed digital circuits and supplemented by a suitable local distribution system. Since no analogue signals have to be handled, the data exchanges could be purely electronic. It is likely that eventually all traffic, speech as well as data, will be in digital form. Digital speech requires a much greater bandwidth than analogue speech and 65

117

kilobits/second is being spoken of as a likely standard for the band-width of a single telephone circuit. We may thus look forward to the time when bandwidths far beyond anything contemplated today will become a matter of normal practice. For a discussion of data communication in relation to public networks, see Allery (1974).

In discussing digital communication systems, communication engineers have come to distinguish between *circuit switching* and *packet switching*. The former would give a service somewhat similar to the existing one based on the telephone network. A user would set up a connection by dialling, or the equivalent, and then have continuous uninterrupted use of the channel that had been provided. Signals would be received at the far end in the same form and at the same speed as they were transmitted, and there would be no time delay other than that of transmission. It would be necessary to make sure before attempting to send data that the terminal at the far end was compatible with the local one as regards speed of operation.

From the transmission point of view, there is a complication in the provision of switched circuits. On the one hand, the user must be able to send and receive any bit pattern that he wishes, while, on the other hand, it must be possible for signals to be transmitted that will be recognised by the network as control signals; for example, it must be possible to send a signal that will break down a connection when it is no longer required. This is sometimes expressed by saying that the circuit must be *transparent* to the transmitted data. In one system that has been proposed, the incoming bit stream is broken up into groups of 8 bits. These are temporarily stored and two extra bits added, one indicating whether the 8 bits with which it is associated are part of the data stream or whether they must be interpreted by the network as a control character, while the other is a synchronising bit. The 10 bits are transmitted by the network which must therefore work at a higher data rate than that of the original data stream; at the far end the two extra bits are removed and, if this is required, the pulses are retimed so that they arrive at a uniform rate. Some details of this system are given by Dell (1971). In an alternative system, in which the unit of transmission is also the 8-bit group, control groups are distinguished from data groups by being preceded by a particular group known as an *escape group* and capable of being recognised by the network (cf. the escape character described on p. 33). If an escape group happens to occur in the data stream, another escape

118

group must be transmitted in front of it. There is no error correction in either of these systems, and if the user wishes to have an error rate better than the error rate of the circuit then he must, himself, provide and utilise the necessary redundancy.

In packet-switching (Davies *et al.*, 1967), information is supplied to the network by the user in packets containing anything from a single byte to several thousand bits, together with an address indicating the destination to which he wishes it to be sent. The system routes the packet to its destination on a store and forward basis, there being a computer at each node that receives the packet, performs any necessary error checking, and routes it on its way. The system is capable of making speed changes and will deliver the packet at a data rate appropriate to the receiving terminal, irrespective of the rate at which it was originally dispatched. For example, a large number of teletype users may feed packets into the network at 110 bits/second and all these packets may eventually find their way into the same distant computer through a single line working at a data rate of, say, 48 kilobits/second. Since parity checks can be made at each node, and repetition demanded if necessary, packet-switching enables a much better error rate to be guaranteed than does circuit switching.

It is to be noted that the computers at the nodes are fully dedicated to the operation of the network, and are not available for performing any operations on the data that they handle other than those associated with transmission. A packet-switching system is intended to operate under such conditions that the delay caused by storage at the nodes is inappreciable. If the receiving terminal is unavailable, the network will abandon the package. A packet-switching system is to be distinguished from a *hold and forward* system, which is capable of holding messages, if necessary for several hours or days, until they can be delivered.

Experience with packet-switching has so far been confined to organisations that have set up systems for their own purposes using rented telephone lines. Telegraph and telephone administrations are now considering the possibility of providing a public packet-switching service. The United Kingdom Post Office has plans at an advanced stage of implementation for establishing an experimental packet-switching system. Both a packet-switching system and a circuit-switching system could be supported by the same underlying data transmission network. In considering the relative merits of circuit-switching and packet-switching, one must bear in mind that the set-up time in a digital circuit switching system would be very short, perhaps 100 milliseconds. This suggests that an alternative to packet-switching would be a circuit-switching system used in such a way that connections were very frequently established and broken down. However, packet-switching has very real merits from the point of view of computer users, particularly in the facilities it provides for data rate changing. There are signs that, partly as a result of the success of the private systems referred to above, these merits are now becoming more generally recognised in communication circles.

Packet-switching networks

The Advanced Research Projects Agency has established an extensive network, known as the ARPA net, which links many of the universities and other organisations that it supports throughout the United States, and has extensions to the United Kingdom and Norway (L. G. Roberts, 1970). The ARPA network is based exclusively on packet-switching. It makes available to all the participating organisations facilities which exist only in one place and which are not readily transportable. Not only do these include experimental computer systems such as ILLIAC 4, but they also include large software systems such as MACSYMA which runs on MULTICS at M.I.T. Formerly, such software systems were only available at one place until, if ever, they reached the stage of development at which the time and effort required to make them transportable became justified. The emphasis is thus on making collaboration in research possible, rather than on sharing load. The philosophy is to exploit the variety in the facilities available and not to try to standardise them.

The ARPA net functions strictly as a communication network. It puts a user in touch with the distant computer, which he can then use on exactly the same terms as a local user; unless he merely wishes to use a 'guest' facility available freely to all applicants, he must have the necessary authorisation to log-in and must understand the procedure to use. For serious use he requires documentation for the distant system, but in the case of most systems a HELP command has been implemented that provides the minimum information necessary for using the system.

At each node on the ARPA net is a computer known as an *interface message processor* (IMP). The IMPs are all Honeywell computers type DDP 516 with 12K words of memory, part of which is of a protected read-only type. The IMP programs are all identical with the exception of one word containing the identity of the node. They are permanently interconnected to form a network by means of full duplex channels having a bandwidth of 50 kilobits/sec. An IMP may have up to four computers (usually situated close by) connected to it. A computer so connected is said to act as a *host* to the IMP. The program in the host that is responsible for communication with the IMP is known as the *network control program* (NCP); this is closely related to the host operating system and responsibility for writing it rests with the management of the host computer. Writing an NCP has proved a challenging task even for an expert system programmer. It is possible for the NCP to be located not in the host computer itself, but in a satellite to it, provided that good communication facilities exist between the satellite and the main computer.

The IMP receives a message containing up to 8K bits for transmission to a given destination. The IMP breaks the message up into packets each containing up to 1K data bits, with which are associated 150 bits for destination, source, redundancy, etc. A feature of the ARPA net is dynamic routing. Normally a packet is forwarded by the most direct route but, if congestion occurs or if a line becomes unserviceable, the packet can travel by an alternative route. It can sometimes happen that consecutive packets of a message go by different routes. The packets carry serial numbers so that the receiving IMP can assemble them correctly into a reconstituted message that it passes to the receiving host. On receipt of a packet an IMP checks the redundancy and if this is correct acknowledges the packet. If no acknowledgement is received within a certain time, the sending IMP transmits the packet afresh and continues to do this until the acknowledgment is finally received.

Communication between the various modules of hardware and software that make up the ARPA net system is governed by a series of *protocols*. A protocol is a set of conventions covering in detail the exact manner in which the information is formatted and transmitted; the term is also loosely used to refer to a program which embodies the conventions. The lowest-level protocol governs the way in which packets are exchanged between IMPs, with error checking and re-

121

transmission as described above. If an IMP has no packet to transmit, it exchanges dummy messages with its neighbours at half-second intervals, so that any trouble on the line will become apparent.

In the host the first-level protocol specifies the way in which messages are passed to the IMP for transmission to a distant host and vice-versa. The NCP must be written so as to observe this protocol. The second-level protocol in the host is concerned with the logical interchange of information between NCPs in communicating hosts. This protocol introduces the concept of links between communicating hosts; these links are always established as a preliminary to the interchange of messages. They are entirely virtual and are introduced partly for reasons of conceptual clarity and partly as a device to prevent the IMP being flooded with information; this is achieved by establishing the convention that only one message at a time may pass through a given link. Third-level protocols govern communication between processes in hosts and cover initial connection, file transfer, remote job entry, and the interfacing of user terminals. The program for the latter is known as TELNET. A teletype or other similar terminal can be connected direct to a process in its own host *via* the multiplexer and operating system; in this case it has nothing to do with the ARPA net. Alternatively it can be connected to the TELNET program (again through the multiplexer) and thence to a process either in the same host or in a distant one. TELNET enables remote and local terminals to present exactly the same interface to a process. It also handles code conversion so as to accommodate a wide range of terminals. This useful facility costs only 1 K words and makes it unnecessary to impose on users irksome restrictions as to the terminal that they should choose.

A user wishing to be connected to a time-sharing system in a distant host proceeds as follows. He first logs-in to his own host and establishes connection with TELNET. He then types @ followed by the network serial number of the host he wishes to use. @ is an escape character that enables the user to communicate with his local TELNET program whenever he needs to do so during the subsequent dialogue. The TELNET program ascertains whether the distant host is available and if so sets up a pair of links, one go and one return. A message to this effect appears on the user's terminal. He is now in exactly the same position as if he had been a local user logging-in to the host. He can even use the TELNET program in that host to establish contact with a third host.

The procedure is even simpler if the user's terminal is connected to what is known as a terminal IMP or a TIP. This is an IMP with an additional 8K words of core used to hold programs that perform the more essential of the functions performed by the NCP and TELNET programs found in a host. These enable the TIP to support terminals directly. If a user with a terminal connected to a TIP wishes to use the TENEX system at BBN (for example) he types @ L 69, 69 being the network serial number of that computer. After a brief interval, if the computer is available he receives a message to the effect that the links to it are open. He then goes ahead to log-in. It would hardly be possible to imagine a simpler procedure.

Since the part of the TIP that acts as a host is limited in capacity, the services that the TIP can offer to a user at a directly connected console are also limited. A significant advance came with the realisation that a TIP, or any other small host, could be programmed so that it would call on a larger host somewhere on the system for assistance in dealing with requests that it could not itself meet. Such a request might, for example, be to supply information about the system and the users connected to it. As the facility is implemented, a TIP on receiving such a request, will first locate a 'friendly' host, obtain the required information, and pass it to the user. The host, in practice, is one of a number of PDP10 computers connected to the net and all operating under the TENEX operating system.

There are, at present, about 12 PDP10s with TENEX on the net and these may be regarded as forming a homogeneous network within the ARPA net. The facility described in the last paragraph has made possible an interesting and successful experiment in providing a *network supervisor* that makes it possible to treat the PDP10s as a single resource. A user anywhere on the net may request service from a TENEX system and his local TELNET program will make contact with a copy of the network supervisor running in one of the PDP10s. The network supervisor will then connect the user to a TENEX system that is prepared to accept him. Facilities can also be provided whereby information filed in one TENEX is readily available in another; in other words, the separate filing systems are brought together to form one large system. This experiment may, perhaps, point the way in which computers within a homogeneous network

123

can be controlled as a whole. It should, however, be noted that what made the experiment possible was the availability of the general communication features of the ARPA net. In the case of a homogeneous network composed of a set of directly connected computers, these facilities would have to be specially provided.

It was pointed out in Chapter 2 that, in a full duplex system, characters typed by the user may be echoed either by the multiplexer routine or by the system or object program with which he is working. In some circumstances no echo at all is required. This problem takes on an additional dimension when a computer network is being used since there are then more places from which the echo might come. For example, it might come from the local computer, from the communication software in the distant computer, or from the object program in the distant computer with which the terminal user is communicating. In the latter case the echo need not be an exact replica of what is sent. The ARPA net gives the user the option of requesting, by messages addressed to his local TELNET, either local or remote echoing. It also enables him to determine whether the characters shall be sent one by one as they are typed, whether they shall be sent in groups—for example, a line at a time—or whether they shall be sent whenever the local buffer is full. If they are sent singly, each character requires the transmission of a packet composed of 158 bits of which only 8 represent the character. Remote echoing character by character calls for the return of a similar-sized packet for each character typed. This low proportion of data bits is not as serious a matter as it sounds because characters typed by users—few of whom make very many key strokes per hour—form a small part of the traffic handled by the ARPA net. The more voluminous information returned by computers to users is packed much more densely into packets, and so is material transmitted according to the file transfer and remote job entry protocols.

TYMSHARE Inc. has established a network known as TYMNET whose primary purpose is to connect users to the time-sharing service that it provides (Tymes, 1971). Switching computers at the nodes are known as TYMSATS and are inter-connected by means of voice grade lines. The TYMSATS, like the IMPs, work on the store and forward principle, but there is a difference in that all packets (known as logical records) exchanged between a terminal and a distant computer pass along the same route. The route is defined by

124

table entries in the software of the TYMSATS concerned and is set up when the user first logs in. This function is performed by a network supervisor that runs in one or other of the computers that provide the time-sharing service. One advantage of storing the routing information within the network is that packets do not have to carry destination addresses with them. On the other hand, if an equipment failure occurs, the services of the supervisor are necessary to set up alternative paths for users who have been affected. The network supervisor maintains full information about the state of the network. If the computer in which it is running fails, another supervisor, running in another computer, takes over, first interrogating the TYMSATS to find out what the network status is.

Packets are grouped together for transmission between TYMSATS into physical records and redundancy is added for error control. The TYMSAT economises in transmission overheads by collecting together into the same physical record packages originating from different terminals but intended for the same destination.

The echo is normally provided by the TYMSAT to which a user is connected and hence is virtually instantaneous; however, the TYMSAT is programmed so as to recognise circumstances in which an immediate echo would be an embarrassment, for example, when information is being printed on the user's terminal and he is typing ahead. It then stops echoing itself and instructs the distant computer to provide the echo instead. When the user stops typing, the TYMSAT resumes the echoing role, first sending signals to find out whether it is safe for it to do so; the criteria are that the distant program should be waiting for the user to type further characters and that there should be no characters on their way to his terminal for printing.

7 Filing Systems

Modern filing systems, that handle information independently of its significance in any particular context, all derive from that designed by Corbató for the CTSS. A brief description of that system was given in Chapter 2. The material of the present chapter is based largely on the work of A. G. Fraser in Cambridge.

The name given in Cambridge to the program which controls the filing system is *file master*. The first step in the design of a file master is to arrive at a satisfactory allocation system for space on the disc. This space is divided into blocks, the length of which depends on the particular disc file used; in a typical case, a block consists of 512 computer words. In a computer with paging, it is highly desirable that the sizes of pages and blocks, if not equal, should be simply related. If files were of fixed length, then an easy and efficient procedure would be to allocate a number of consecutive blocks to each file. Since, however, files vary in length dynamically, it is necessary to use a chaining technique of the type familiar in list processing. In the simplest form of this technique, one or two words in each block are used to contain the link, the rest containing data. Initially, all the blocks on the disc are chained together to form a free list. Blocks may be taken from this list when new files are being created, or existing files extended, and they may similarly be returned when they are no longer required.

A preferable system is to maintain a table, or *storage map*, containing an entry for each block on the disc. Chaining of blocks is then done by means of appropriate entries in the storage map and not by recording links in the blocks themselves. This has the advantage that administration of the blocks can be performed without accessing them. Administration in this sense includes setting up the free list in the first place, returning blocks to it when they are no longer needed, locating particular blocks in a multi-block file, and checking the consistency of the filing system after a failure has occurred. With some hardware systems, there is a further advantage in not having to use any of the words in a block to contain links. This is the case in the

126

Atlas 2 system where the block is 512 words, both on the disc and on magnetic tape; it would be rather inconvenient if disc blocks contained only 510 words.

A disc map normally occupies several thousand computer words and is rather large to keep permanently in the memory. It can, however, be divided into sections, and if there is some sort of paging, software-simulated or otherwise, then there is a good chance of the part of the map required being available in core.

The problem of organising space on a drum is very similar to that of organising space on a disc, and much of what has been said about discs applies equally well to drums. Indeed, if a system is equipped with both a disc and a drum, there is everything to be said for the principle that all space on the drum, other than that used for swapping or for holding parts of the supervisor that are not permanently resident in core, should be treated as far as possible in the same way as space on the disc, and handled by a common system. This means that the system can put a file equally well on the disc, or on the drum; it is, in fact, a user or management decision where a particular file goes, the decision being taken on considerations of response time and economics. It is to be understood that, in what follows, references to a disc can, in general, be interpreted as though they were references to a drum, and vice versa.

It might be thought that there is no case for allowing an individual file to be partly on the disc and partly on a drum. However, it was pointed out on p. 94 that when a file is loaded as a segment in a computer with a virtual memory one of the possible swapping strategies that could be adopted would cause pages that were originally on the disc to be transferred to the drum. It is possible that this somewhat messy situation could be more elegantly handled if the file master were so designed that some pages of a file could be on drum and some on discs. The fact that a file were so divided would then be a private matter for the file master; from the point of view of the rest of the system, the file would be in every way a normal file. There would be a housekeeping routine associated with the file master that would tidy up a given file by transferring to the disc any pages that were on the drum. This routine could be activated at fixed intervals of time, or when drum space became tight. Various algorithms suggest themselves for choosing files to be treated; factors to be taken into account are the amount of drum space available, the relative loading of disc,

127

drum and core channels and what, if anything, is known about the manner in which a particular file is accessed.

Once the technical problem of space allocation has been suitably solved, attention may be given to designing the file directories, of which there must be one for each user, and the interfaces between the file master and the other modules of the supervisor. When suitably requested, the file master must put an object program (or a system program) in touch with the right file belonging to the right user, and it must ensure the privacy of the files belonging to the individual users. If the users are entirely independent of each other, there is no particular problem about privacy. In a practical system, however, the following additional requirements arise. It must be possible for one user to authorise another user to have access to certain of his files. It must also be possible for users working in groups to share a set of files between them as well as having their own personal files.

There are two ways in which the mutual use of files may be accomplished. The owner of a file may be required to take keyboard action himself to authorise another user; he may be able, for example, to set up a list of people privileged to use his files with details of their privileges. Alternatively, the owner may make it possible for another user to have access to one or more of his files by disclosing to that user a secret key or password which he may then type himself. The former of these methods would appear to be most suitable for users working together in groups on the same problem, and the latter for the casual sharing of files in a computer community.

File directories

In designing a system of file directories, it is natural to begin by thinking in terms of a hierarchy, the entries in the higher-level directories being other directories, and the entries in the lower-level directories being a mixture of files and directories, with files alone at the lowest level of all. Such a system enables the needs of users who work in groups and subgroups to be catered for very conveniently. It is, however, often necessary for users to have access to files owned by other users situated in quite different parts of the hierarchy; in the interests of efficiency of access, therefore, it is desirable to provide for the establishment of direct links from one user's directory to

128

another user's files. Daley and Neumann (1965) have described a system in which this is done.

During the normal operation of a time-sharing system very frequent references are made to files. Some of these references are explicitly called for by the user; others are references made by the system, or by a subsystem, and some of these may be to files of which the user is not aware. It is important, therefore, to design the filing system in such a way that the operations of opening, closing, and accessing files can be done in the minimum of time, and in-practice this means with a minimum number of accesses to the drum or disc on which the directories are held. An excessive number of disc accesses in the opening and closing of files, particularly system files, can ruin the performance of a system. Indeed, this is often the reason for sluggish response in time-sharing systems in which the design of the filing system has been approached from a formal point of view rather than from the point of view of the implementer. The first principle should be to keep to a minimum the number of hierarchically organised directories that must be consulted in order to obtain access to a file.

In the Cambridge file master there were only two levels of file directory. The master directory which was regarded as the property of the system contained references to directories belonging to users. These directories in turn contained references to individual files, and also to information that the system needed to have, or could usefully have, about the files. The former category of information included the name of a file, whether it was permanent or temporary, and what type of access other users were allowed to have to it. In the latter category might be information about when the file was last used and how often it had been accessed.

Since there were only two levels, it was feasible to access files on all occasions *via* the master directory so that the problems associated with the following of links were avoided. Any process could initiate the process of accessing a file belonging to another user. Only when the file master had located the file requested did it proceed to examine the applicant's credentials. Two separate sets of conditions were taken into account: (1) general limitations that might have been placed on the use of the file by its owner and, (2) privileges accorded to, or disabilities imposed upon, the particular user or process requesting access. Sometimes these privileges might override the

129

user's instructions; for example, the process responsible for dumping files on to magnetic tapes for purposes of integrity had an absolute right of access to files for this purpose.

The various checks necessary to validate a request for file access can be done in an *ad hoc* fashion by suitable orders incorporated in the programs, but there are advantages in handling them by a uniform method. Such a method was devised by Fraser and is described on pp. 132–6; it comprises a simple system of book-keeping for recording and updating authorities for the various actions, and a procedure for ascertaining in given circumstances whether a particular action is legitimate or not.

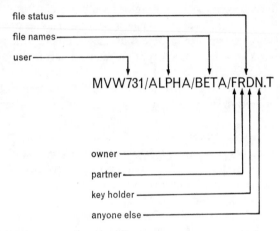

F free access
D power to delete, change status, or read
C power to change status, or read
R power to read only
L power to load for execution only (programs)
N no access

Fig. 7.1

The CTSS introduced the idea of multi-part file names, This was followed in the Cambridge system. Every file had a name consisting of three parts (see Fig. 7.1). The first part identified the owner and the second and third parts were chosen by the user at will. When a user was referring to his own files he did not need to type the first part. A fourth section might be appended to a file name when the file was first created; this section gave what was known as the *status* of the file. The first letter in this part indicated the privileges that the user gave himself in relation to the file. The second was used to indicate the privileges that he gave to *partners* of whom he would have to supply a list; this feature was intended for the benefit of programmers working together in a group on the same project. The third letter was used to indicate the privileges given to *keyholders*, that is, users who had been told a secret keyword which they could quote in order to obtain access to a file. The fourth letter indicated the privileges given to anyone else. In the example given in Fig. 7.1 the owner is free to do what he likes with the file, a partner can only read it, a keyholder can delete it, change its status, or read it, while any other user is allowed no access at all. If, when creating a file, the user omitted the status letters then a default setting would operate. The system would prevent a user creating a file that he could neither delete nor change in status; by giving a file status C he could, however, protect himself against deleting it accidentally.

Keyholders were more often programs than people. The facility enabled a user to be given access to a confidential file but only *via* a certain program. The program would have the keyword embedded in it and the user would be given load only access to the file in which it was contained. When the user ran the program it would 'quote' the keyword and obtain access to the file. The user himself would have no direct access to the file at all.

The first group of status digits was terminated by a dot. A letter T after the dot indicated that the file was a temporary one and a letter P indicated that it was permanent. Temporary files existed only on the disc, while permanent files were automatically copied by the system on to magnetic tape, usually within twenty minutes of their creation. Magnetic tape was used in this way both to provide security against loss of information on account of system failure. and also to provide overflow for file storage. A file marked with the letter A (for *archive*) after the dot normally resided on magnetic tape and was only brought on to the disc when its presence was specifically requested by the user. This he did by changing its class to P.

In most systems separate commands are provided for typing out the file directory, deleting a file, and changing the access status of a file. The Cambridge Multiple Access System introduced the idea of the interactive editing of a file directory. The user would give the command EXAMINE and this would cause the machine to print out his file directory line by line. After printing the particulars of each file, the machine would wait for the user to type any instructions that he might have to give. The word DELETE would cause the file to be deleted and the system would respond by printing the word DELETED. It would then pass on to print particulars of the next file. If the user had forgotten what was in a file, he could have a copy typed out there and then by typing the word TYPE. If the user had no instructions to give, he would merely type a carriage return and the system would pass on to the next file.

If the user simply typed the word EXAMINE as above, the machine would go systematically through his entire directory, printing full information about each file, including the amount of space occupied, the date the file was originally created, whether in the case of a permanent file it had yet been dumped on to magnetic tape and, if so, the name of the tape on which it could be found. By typing the word TITLES, either after the command name or when-ever the machine paused for instructions, he could request that file names only were printed: similarly the word LIST would cause the machine to print a copy of the directory without pausing for instruc-tions. The command EXAMINE could be followed by the name of a particular file, in which case particulars of that file only would be printed. Similarly, a user could specify that only entries relating to files belonging to the same group—that is, having a given first part to their names—should be printed. Compared with the use of separate commands for listing and deleting files, or changing their access status, the use of an interactive EXAMINE command saves the user much time and trouble.

Since most users will not, at any given time, use quite all the filing space on the disc allocated to them, the management can safely allocate more than is physically available. Features such as those just described that make it easy for the user to edit his file directory, are therefore, important to the system, since they help to prevent space on the disc being wasted by files that are no longer required.

Control of file access

The system for controlling file access, implemented by Fraser for the Cambridge multiple-access system, is described here in a somewhat streamlined version. The basis of the system is the *authority list* which contains a series of independent and free-standing statements to the effect that, if certain conditions are satisfied, then a specified set of actions are allowed. Each entry in the authority list is called an *authority*. For convenience, there is one global authority list and one authority list associated with each file directory, no matter whether that directory is the property of a user or of some system facility such as the library.

Authorities are of two forms; one concerns the accessing of files that already exist, and the other concerns such actions as creating a new file, making an entry in a file directory, putting a file directory for a new user into the system, making changes in an authority list, and performing various actions concerned with the dumping and reloading of files.

An authority consists of a Boolean function, B_i, whose value depends on the status of the user or program requesting access, and a Boolean vector with one component corresponding to each of the various actions that can be requested. The Boolean vector is, in fact, implemented as a binary word, with the digits corresponding to actions; a digit has the value 1 if the action is allowed, and 0 if it is not.

For reasons of implementation, some restrictions must be placed on the form taken by the Boolean function, B_i. In the system being described, it is restricted to be a product of not more than four of the primitive Boolean functions listed below; only two of the four functions may have arguments. Each function takes the value 1 if the condition associated with it is satisfied, and 0 otherwise. These restrictions enable B_i to be coded into a few computer words only.

$p_1(X) = 1$ if name of user is X

$p_2(X) = 1$ if user has quoted key X

$p_3(X) = 1$ if user has specified X as the second part of a file name

$p_4(X) = 1$ if user is working at console X

$p_5(X) = 1$ if user has given command X

$p_6 = 1$ if user has quoted his password correctly

$p_7 = 1$ if user is working at a console

$p_8 = 1$ if user is not working at a console

$p_9 = 1$ unconditionally

The binary word associated with an authority for accessing an

133

existing file will be denoted by a_i. The first five digits of a_i correspond to the actions of write, delete, change status, read, load; the three following groups of five digits correspond to the same actions in the same order. Thus the same action can be authorised by the occurrence of a 1 in any or all of four places. The four groups of five digits correspond to the four status letters (owner, partner, keyholder, and others) of Fig. 7.1, but this identification is a consequence of the way the system is used rather than of the way that it is constructed.

Examples of authorities that would appear in the authority list associated with the file directory belonging to a user called JACK are as follows:

$$p_1(\text{JACK})\, p_6 \quad 11111 \ 00000 \ 00000 \ 00000 \qquad (1)$$

This gives authority for JACK to access a file in any manner provided that he has given his password correctly.

$$p_9 \qquad\qquad 00000 \ 00000 \ 00000 \ 11111 \qquad (2)$$

This gives authority for anyone to access the file.

$$p_2(\text{LET}) \qquad 00000 \ 00000 \ 00011 \ 00000 \qquad (3)$$

This gives authority for a keyholder who has typed the keyword LET to read or load files (that is to have access with status letter R).

$$p_1(\text{JOHN}) \qquad 00000 \ 01111 \ 00000 \ 00000 \qquad (4)$$

This gives authority for JOHN to have access as a partner with status D.

The first two of these authorities would appear in the user's authority list when the user is first established in the system. The others would be placed there as a result of his creating a keyholder and a partner. It is through authorities such as these that the four groups of five digits become associated with owner, partner, keyholder, and others.

This, however, is not the whole story, since effect has to be given to restrictions that the owner of a file may place on it. Associated with each file is another binary word also containing four groups of five digits each. These are status words set up by the owner of the files and a typical one will be denoted by s. In the case of the file illustrated in Fig. 7.1, for example, the status word would be

$$11111 \ 00011 \ 01111 \ 00000$$

corresponding to the status FRDN. Finally, there is a request word, r, created by a user program, or a system program working on behalf of a user, when access to a file is required. This also has four groups of five binary digits, and there is a 1 in each of these groups in the position corresponding to the action requested. For example, a request to read a file would be

$$00010 \ 00010 \ 00010 \ 00010$$

The system works as follows. The B_i are evaluated in turn and the Boolean sum $\Sigma B_i a_i$ is formed. This gives a resultant authority word that contains a 1 in the position corresponding to each action that is authorised by one or other of the authorities that are valid for the user in question at the particular time that the request is made. The system next forms $rs\Sigma B_i a_i$, where digit by digit Boolean multiplication (logical AND) is implied. If this quantity is non-zero the action can go ahead; otherwise a failure is signalled.

The binary word associated with the second type of authority (for performing actions other than accessing existing files) will be denoted by b_i; the complete authority may then be written $B_i b_i$. Such an authority is treated in the same way as the other form of authority except that a status word does not exist and the resultant authority word is formed by evaluating $r\Sigma B_i b_i$. Authorities of the two types are stored in the same lists, but there is a marker digit that enables them to be distinguished.

A few examples will now be given of features that can be readily implemented given the system of authorities that has been described. Authority (1) given above enables a user to have access to his files, provided that he has given his password correctly. If, for some reason, it is desired to allow him to use his files for an off-line job without giving his password, but to retain the password for work done from a console, it is only necessary to add the additional authority

$$p_1(\text{JACK}) \, p_8 \quad 11111 \ 00000 \ 00000 \ 00000$$

Authorities may be used to establish a system whereby users may send messages to one another. Two things are necessary. One is that there should be a system program actuated by the command SIGNAL (say), which will cause a message typed by one user to be placed in a file having MAILBOX (say) for the first part of its name in the file directory of another user, creating such a file if it does not already exist. The second user must, however, have indicated that he

135

is willing to receive such messages, and this he does by causing two authorities to be included in his authority list. The first allows the SIGNAL command to have access to an existing file called MAILBOX and is as follows:

$$p_5(\text{SIGNAL})\, p_3(\text{MAILBOX}) \quad 10010\ 00000\ 00000\ 00000$$

The other authority is of the second kind; it has the same Boolean function and gives authority for the creation of a file.

All users have authority to add to or amend their own authority lists. Similar rights are automatically accorded to any partners that a user may establish with free access to his files. In order to introduce a new authority, a user types the command RELATION, followed by a specification of the authority to be set up; for example, if a user wishes to authorise all console users to have access to a particular group of his files, then he would type

RELATION NNNF IF ON-LINE AND GROUP = RECORDS

This would authorise access to any file having RECORDS as the second part of its name. In addition to the general command for setting up authorities, there are special commands for setting up authorities of particular types, for example those relating to partners and keyholders.

The method of authorities would appear capable of development into a general system for according privileges to users and programs that need them. The reader may care to ponder on the relationship between this approach and the one that was discussed on p.72 *et seq.*

Character and binary files

There are, from the point of view of the user, two types of file, character files, and binary files. A character file contains a string of symbols such as appear on a typewriter. Files created in the manner just described are character files, and the incoming characters are converted to a standard internal code by the multiplexer routine. When a character file is connected to a program *via* the file master, it acts very much as an input or output device, delivering or receiving characters one at a time. Character files are, in fact, associated with functions that in earlier days would have been performed by primary input or output. The necessary packing into computer words for

136

storage on the disc, and the corresponding unpacking, is performed by systems routines, and takes place behind the scenes as far as the programmer is concerned.

A binary file contains information ready for direct loading into core. Many binary files will, in fact, be dumped programs, or parts of programs. Although there is a clear distinction between character files and binary files, the format in which files are stored by the file master should be completely context free; that is, it should not be possible to tell (other than by the methods of cryptography) from an examination of the file itself to which category it belongs. If files are marked in the file directory as being either character or binary, then this should be regarded as a service to the programmer to help him avoid confusing them unwittingly. There should be nothing that will prevent him from creating a file as a character file and using it as a binary file, or vice versa. To be able to do this, he must, of course, be provided with information about the form in which character files are stored, including details of the internal code and of the way in which characters are packed into computer words.

Buffering

When a file is being used by a program, it is not usually necessary that the whole file should be loaded into core at the same time and, in the case of long files, this would, in any case, be impossible. A buffering problem, therefore, arises. If programs are normally run to completion once they have been loaded into core, that is if swapping is the exception rather than the rule, then input buffering can be done wholly in space available to the supervisor. If a program is swapped out of memory, any information being buffered on its behalf is abandoned and when the program returns to memory the buffer is re-filled. If a good deal of swapping takes place, it is better that the buffer space should be regarded as part of the user's working space, although it is used not by his program but by the supervisor, and the long arm of the supervisor extends to prevent him from accidentally writing into it. The advantage of treating the buffer as a part of the user's space is that, when the user's program is swapped out of core, anything in the buffer goes with it and automatically returns when the program returns.

A similar buffering problem arises when a character file receives output from a program. In this case, the necessary buffer space is probably better regarded as belonging to the supervisor. Once information has reached the buffer, it is beyond the reach of the program, and the supervisor can write it into the file at any time that the space occupied by the buffer is needed for some other purpose.

In the case of a machine based on a virtual memory, buffering for binary files can be provided automatically by the paging system. The programmer merely attaches his file as a segment to his program, and individual pages from it are brought into core as required. Character files can be dealt with in the same way, packing and unpacking into characters being done by a system routine or, if these operations are extremely simple, as they are in a computer that works with 8-bit addressable bytes, by a system macro. Unless pages of a small size can be used, however, considerations of efficiency may render it inexpedient to use an automatic paging system for buffering small quantities of information. This remark applies even more to the buffering of information from teletypes than to the buffering required in accessing a character file.

File names and the avoidance of clashes

When access is first required to a file, an appeal must be made by the user program to the file master. The file is referred to by its full alphanumeric name, including the name of the directory in which it is to be found. The file master checks that the file exists and that access is permitted. It then passes information about the file and the user concerned to the supervisor. The file is then said to be *open* and the user program may make future references to it by calling on the supervisor. The supervisor maintains a list of the files that are open in this way, together with a direct reference to the number of the record on the disc where the file is to be found. If the file extends over more than one record on the disc, this reference is updated as the file is worked through, use being made of the storage map for this purpose. Once a file is open, it is not necessary for a user program to refer to it by its full alphanumeric name; instead, it can be referred to by a number giving its position in the list.

When the Cambridge multiple-access system was developed, it was

138

possible to make use of a system of stream numbers already provided by the supervisor for dealing with input and output and for transfers to and from magnetic tape. Under this system, the programmer writes his program so as to take inputs from *input streams*, and to send outputs to *output streams*. The connection of these streams to physical input and output devices, or to magnetic tape, is effected not by the program, but by a preliminary job description. This system was easily extended to make it possible to connect streams to files.

The advantage of proceeding in this way is that the program can be written entirely in terms of streams, leaving until later the specification of where information comes from or where information goes to. Thus, by writing appropriate job descriptions, a program can be fed with information from a document read in from a tape reader, typed on a console, or taken from a file; and similarly for output. The request to the file master to open a file is made when the job description is processed, and this necessary procedure is thus completely divorced from the accessing of the file by the program.

It will be appreciated that, since an ordinary user writes many programs over a period of time and creates many files, some system such as that outlined is absolutely necessary in order to avoid name clashes. If programs had written into them the actual names of files that they require, and if different programs used the same names with different meanings, then much confusion could result. At the best, much tedious renaming of files would be necessary.

MULTICS identifies files and segments; a given object may be described sometimes in its life cycle as a file, and at other times as a segment, but it is regarded as possessing a continuous identity, and the programmer always refers to it by its name, or by one of its names if it has more than one. When incorporated in a process, a segment is referred to by the position that the entry relating to it occupies in the segment table; this is, in effect, a temporary name, although it is one of which the programmer is unaware.

The recovery and archive problems

The amount of space on the disc file will inevitably be limited and it is necessary to provide some mechanism whereby files can overflow on to magnetic tape and be recalled at will by the user. It is also necessary to provide a system whereby information that has been lost from the disc as a result of system failure can be reinstated. This also depends on the use of magnetic tape. Although the archive and recovery problems are logically distinct, it is natural that a common solution to them should be sought. The system evolved will be conditioned by the frequency and nature of the system failures that are encountered on a particular installation, and on the amount of disc space available in relation to users' requirements. There are many conflicting requirements to be reconciled, and it is unlikely that any completely general solution to these two problems will ever be reached.

The simplest procedure is to dump the entire contents of the disc on to magnetic tape at fixed intervals of time. Unfortunately, the dumping of a large disc is a lengthy operation and could hardly be undertaken more frequently than once a week. This would mean that when a system failure occurred users would lose up to a week's work. An alternative is to dump on to tape within a short interval of their having been created all new or modified files. This is known as *incremental dumping*. In principle, either of the above two systems enables information that has been erased from the disc, either deliberately or accidentally, to be reinstated. The dump tapes will, however, contain, in addition to current information, a great deal of material that is no longer of value, namely, old versions of files, files that users wish to have purged from the system, and old file directories. It is therefore necessary to have some system for editing the dump tapes. If users are allowed to pass information into the archives in an unrestricted manner, the editing problem can become acute as the number of dump tapes increases. If, however, the amount of archive space available to users is regarded as being limited—at any rate for the time being—this uncontrolled growth is avoided. If, at a later time, it becomes necessary to increase the amount of archive space, steps can be taken to make sure that the editing procedures available are adequate for the purpose. Archive space should be regarded as a system resource to be allocated like other resources.

Whatever system is adopted, a record must be kept of where copies of all files that are of current value are to be found on the dump tapes. The logical place to keep this information is in the file directories of the individual owners of the files. This implies that files that have been relegated to the archive system should still appear in the file directories, a principle which is, in any case, sound, in order that a user may be kept aware of what files he possesses. A record must also be kept of where on tape is the latest version of each file directory. Users sometimes delete files accidentally, and demand to have them reinstated. Since there is inevitably a longish interval before deleted files are finally purged from the dump tapes, there is no reason why such requests should not be granted. For use on this and on other occasions when administrative intervention is necessary, it is convenient to have a listing showing where all files and file directories are to be found on the dump tapes.

Neither full dumping of the disc nor incremental dumping is likely by itself to be wholly satisfactory and, as an example of schemes that may be considered, the following one devised by A. G. Fraser for use in Cambridge may be of interest. There are two sets of magnetic tapes, each used cyclically; they will be referred to respectively as the primary and secondary cycles. Each tape cycle holds part of the information that is in the system. All files marked by the user P (permanent) and A (archive) are dumped; purely temporary files are not dumped. For every P and A file, the relevant file directory contains a note as to whether or not the file has yet been dumped on to magnetic tape and, if so, a statement of whereabouts in the primary or secondary cycle the copy is to be found.

Tapes in the primary cycle are used for incremental dumping. The incremental dumping routine runs approximately every 20 minutes and, while it is running, one tape—the current tape—from the primary cycle must be mounted on the computer. All new and changed files are dumped on to the current tape at the first opportunity, and the file directory is annotated accordingly. When a tape in the primary cycle comes to be re-used, there may well be on it information that is still of value, but has not yet found its way on to one of the secondary tapes. The system automatically re-dumps such information on to the current tape and updates the record in the file directory.

The routine responsible for administering the secondary cycle runs at arbitrarily chosen intervals. Two tapes from the secondary cycle must be mounted on the computer—the tape on to which information is being written, which will be referred to as tape A, and the last tape in the cycle, which is used in a read only manner and will be referred to as tape Z. When the operations now being described have been completed, tape Z will become available for re-use.

141

The secondary cycle routine scans the file directories and copies on to tape A all P and A files that have not so far been dumped on to the secondary cycle; the entries corresponding to these files in the file directories are marked accordingly. The routine also copies from tape Z to tape A all files that had been dumped earlier and are still to be found in a file directory with status P or A.

It will be seen that, while the two cycles share the responsibility for storing information, there is no direct connection between them other than that provided by the entries in the file directories. In particular, when a file has been safely dumped on to the secondary cycle and this fact recorded in the file directory, its eventual dropping from the primary cycle follows automatically. If some holdup occurs in the operation of the secondary cycle, the result is simply that more information is re-dumped during the operation of the primary cycle.

There is a further routine associated with the secondary cycle. This runs every few hours. It scans the file directories, and lists all files marked as having been changed from A to P since the last run. These are sorted into order according to their location on the secondary tapes, and the routine causes requests to be typed for the operators to mount these tapes in order that the files may be restored to the disc.

For convenience, the secondary cycle may be divided into five independent cycles, each dealing with one-fifth of the total number of users and being run on a different day in the week. This both spreads out the work that has to be done in operating the system and also helps to diversify the users' risks.

Restarting after system failure

Making it possible for the system to be restarted after a failure with as little loss as possible should be a principal object of the software designer. Even if all software bugs are eventually eliminated, hardware faults will always occur. Clearly, no software system can be entirely protected against hardware failure, but some are better than others. Often, what appear to be simple and straightforward software solutions, which involve a minimum of disc transfers, have to be rejected since the protection they give is not as good as it could be. Restart procedures should be designed into the system from the beginning, and the necessity for the system to spend time in copying vital information from one place to another should be cheerfully accepted. A system will be judged as much by the efficiency of its restart procedures as by the facilities that it provides.

It is good practice in system programming to minimise the time during which the contents of a communication area—or indeed of any area containing system information—are being modified and hence are temporarily inconsistent, since the consequence of a system failure occurring during this time can be serious. Often, when a number of things have to be done, it will be found that one particular order of doing them gives minimum vulnerability.

It is important that, as part of the procedure used to restart the system after a failure, the information in communication areas should be made consistent, even if it is not possible to make sure that it is correct. Otherwise, the system may operate in a crippled form and may, perhaps, eventually be brought to a halt by reason of a software tangle from which recovery is impossible. This remark is particularly important in relation to the file directories and disc storage map. An inconsistency may result in some records on the disc being neither recorded as free nor as belonging to one of the files in a directory. If they are left as they are they will be lost to the system. In the absence of further information as to their identity, the best thing that can be done with such records is to put them on the free list. Many other examples can be given of the way in which inconsistent information can lead to eventual trouble. For example, inconsistent scheduling information can easily cause the supervisor to go into a loop.

The detailed design of recovery procedures is not easy and calls for some imagination. It is necessary to visualise the situation that will exist when various things have gone wrong, and to make allowance for the fact that more than one error may have occurred. It is desirable that, when files are lost from the disc, the operation of reinstating them should be automatic, the operator's role being limited as far as possible to loading magnetic tapes called for by the system.

After a serious stoppage, it may be necessary to throw away all unfiled information and to reload the supervisor. It is, however, to be hoped that the file directories and the files themselves will be intact except, perhaps, for one or two files that were in active use when the stoppage occurred and which may have become corrupted or detached from their file directories. That this has happened may become apparent as a result of the consistency check referred to above. If so, the system can automatically initiate the recovery of the files from the dump tapes. If a file directory has to be reloaded, all files to which it refers must also be reloaded. This is because a dumped directory may contain pointers to space on the disc that has been freed and re-used since the dump was made. The master file directory, however, may be reinstated safely if there has been no change in the user population since it was last dumped. Although it can be discovered during the restarting processes that some files are corrupt, in the case of other files this fact will not become apparent until the owner tries to use them. In such cases, he will have to initiate action for their recovery himself by typing a suitable request.

A serious stoppage will involve the reloading of the master file directory and all the files. A minor stoppage, on the other hand, may leave intact much of the temporary information held on the disc and it may, in consequence, be possible to continue with the loss of no jobs other than those actually in progress when the stoppage occurred.

In the case of serious failures, the statement made above that the operation of restarting should be as automatic as possible must be qualified. In these circumstances, a software specialist who understands the system may be able to determine what has happened and short circuit the full restart procedure. It is desirable, therefore, that the system should type a message to the operators telling them to enlist help if it is available. If help is not available, they simply type the word 'continue' and an automatic restart is initiated.

From time to time, it will prove impossible to read a block of information from a dump tape. It is most important that this should not bring the whole recovery procedure to a halt, and desirable that it should not even call for the intervention of an operator. To this end, records on the tape should be made complete in themselves, and contain information which will identify them to the recovery program. If a block cannot be read, the program simply passes on to the next. If the information exists elsewhere on the same tape, it will in due course be used; if it exists on another tape, that tape will eventually be demanded by the system. Since a system failure may occur at any time, there is no way of being sure that the current incremental dump tape is properly terminated; it is important that the recovery program should be so designed that it will recognise the end of the information on the tape, even though no special terminating symbols appear.

Some redundancy in dumping is desirable. Particularly valuable information, such as file directories, should be recorded in more than one place. It may well be thought worthwhile to keep duplicate dump tapes; for example, in the system just described, tapes in the secondary cycle might be duplicated. The recovery system should be designed, however, so as not to require a perfect tape; it should be able to take what information is readable from one of the tapes and use the duplicate tape to fill in the gaps. One naturally thinks of error correcting methods of recording information in this connection.

In order to facilitate restarting the system after a minor failure, periodic dumps may be made on to a drum of areas in core memory containing current information. This will include the lists held by the co-ordinator, the disc map, and information relating to files that are open, including absolute references to blocks on the disc. If this information is sufficiently complete, it can be used to effect a restart from the point at which it was recorded, subject to one condition, namely, that the absolute references to the disc are still valid. This will not be the case if blocks on the disc have been cleared or reused since the information was dumped. The file master should, therefore, be designed so that no blocks are cleared and put back on to the free list after a dump has been established until it is quite certain that a restart from that dump-point will not be necessary.

Other types of filing systems

Filing systems of the type discussed in this chapter have been developed to meet a specific need, namely to serve the day-to-day purposes of the ordinary user of a time-sharing system. The design assumptions underlying these *user-support filing systems*, as they may be called, is that the files are short and can therefore be accessed by very simple scanning algorithms and, furthermore, that whenever editing is done a fresh copy of the entire file can be created. A system of this type will fail when an attempt is made to use it for holding files that are not short enough to satisfy these conditions, for example, inventories or administrative records of any size. A time-sharing system that is used for administrative purposes, or for information retrieval, is likely therefore to have associated with it one or more filing systems that have been specially designed to meet the needs of particular applications. Such systems, especially if large, are known as *data bases*.

Discussion of data bases in general is outside the scope of this book. Requirements differ widely according to the application and there is at present little in the way of settled theory to guide the designer. Among the parameters that vary from one application to another are size, the amount of activity that takes place, and whether this activity is typically scattered at random or tends to be concentrated in a few predicatable areas. A further consideration is the extent to which growth of the data base is anticipated. In general it may be said that if a data base is to be updated on-line then the requirements for integrity are a good deal more stringent than those for a user-support filing system; it is generally necessary that recently keyed information should be protected, not only such files as are designated by the user as being permanent (see Wilkes, 1972). It is often required that contiguous records belonging to the same file shall be place on contiguous tracks or cylinders so that they can be accessed with a minimum of head movement; this is called *placement control* and conflicts with the efficient use of disc space as promoted, for example, by the system of dynamic storage allocation described on pp. 126–8.

8 Operational and Managerial Aspects of Time-Sharing

The more automatic a system becomes, the more necessary it is that handles should be provided by which the management can control it. The designer of the system software must, therefore, have in mind the needs not only of the users but also of the management. This chapter will be concerned with problems of administration and management, all of which have their software aspects.

Security of the system

It is necessary (a) to protect the system from unauthorised users, (b) to protect users' files and system records from being altered by unauthorised persons, and (c) to protect confidential information from leakage. (a) and (b) are clearly important to all organisations, whereas (c) is more important to some than to others, although there are few organisations who do not have confidential information to protect, even if it is only users' records.

Security measures may be classified under four headings:

Control of access. Access may be controlled by passwords, and perhaps by restricting certain users to certain consoles, or giving them access at certain times only. Passwords, if used, must be carefully guarded and changed frequently; the console printing should be switched off when the user is invited to type his password so that no printed record of it exists on his worksheets. The most vulnerable point of a password system is usually the list of passwords and their owners stored in the computer. A device, due to R. M. Needham, has been implemented at Cambridge which avoids the necessity of having such a list. It is based on what may be termed a one-way cipher. In an ordinary communication cipher, the enciphering and deciphering algorithms are of approximately equal complexity, and take an equal time to operate. This places a severe restriction on the enciphering algorithms that can be used. In a one-way cipher, the enciphering algorithm, which does not have to be complicated, is chosen so that

147

no simple deciphering algorithm exists; deciphering is then only possible by a lengthy trial and error process. In Needham's system, when the user first sets his password, or whenever he changes it, it is immediately subjected to the enciphering process, and it is the enciphered form that is stored in the computer. Whenever the password is typed in response to a demand from the supervisor for the user's identity to be established, it is again enciphered and the result compared with the stored version. It would be of no immediate use to a would-be malefactor to obtain a copy of the list of enciphered passwords, since he would have to decipher them before he could use them. For this purpose, he would need access to a computer and, even if full details of the enciphering algorithm were available, the deciphering process would take a long time. A discussion of the merits of various enciphering algorithms has been given by Purdy (1974).

It is desirable that users should be able to set their own passwords. When a user is first authorised he can be given a password chosen by the management and urged to change it to one of his own choosing as soon as possible. Alternatively, he can be given no password so that on the first occasion he can log in without hindrance. If a user forgets his password, or if it becomes corrupted as a result of system malfunctioning, the manager can unset the password so that the user can log in and start again.

Use of ciphers. Information may be disguised by omitting headings, etc., from confidential files, or by making use of an enciphering program —in this case an ordinary cipher which permits of deciphering. In the latter case, the problem is transformed into one of guarding the cipher.

Computer room security. In the final resort, it must be recognised that the integrity of any system depends on the integrity of people, in this case particularly the people who have access to the computer room. Obviously, one should avoid, as far as possible, allowing any one individual to get into a position whereby he can do harm by himself. Computer room security would be an onerous part of any complete computer security system.

Police action. Although breaches of security cannot always be prevented, their effects can be contained if measures are taken to make sure that, as far as possible, they always come to light. Simple forms of policing can readily be built into the system; for example, whenever a user logs in he can be presented with a statement of when, according to the system records, he last logged out. Management

148

should be presented with daily reports on system use, including information not normally of interest, such as the location of the consoles from which users logged in. Armed with this information, the management is in a position to investigate any suspicious happenings that may be brought to its notice.

In any public discussion on time-sharing, there is usually much interest shown in security. It is a fair question to ask, however, how much security should, or need be, built into a system intended for general use. I would suggest that it is a reasonable challenge to the system designer to require that a system should be incapable of penetration from a console, even when normal system malfunctioning occurs. I believe that any large system should meet this requirement, even if it is intended for university use. Unfortunate misunderstanding and lack of confidence can occur if users think that other users are altering their files, and it is not good for students to get access to the administrative records and increase their own allocations of computer time. If users are allowed to have access to their files when using the computer off-line on a batch basis, and if they are required to quote their passwords, a security problem at once arises, since the decks of punched cards submitted for running must contain those passwords. It is necessary that the reception area where such jobs are received should be kept under supervision. An alternative approach to the problem is not to require the quoting of passwords off-line, but to permit access only to those files for which the user has set up (from a console) an explicit authority for off-line use. The position is easier if users put their own cards through the card reader as they do in most cafeteria systems. It is desirable, however, that the passwords should be checked, or at any rate enciphered, immediately so that they do not remain for any length of time within the system in clear. In some organisations it may not be thought worthwhile to exercise any control at all over the off-line use of files. Experience will show what system is the best to adopt in given circumstances. The designers of the Cambridge system endeavoured to give the user some choice in the matter by enabling him, whenever he set or changed his password, to specify whether or not his files were to be available off-line, and whether quoting of the password was to be necessary.

The system manager and his assistants need to have access to the system for the purpose of setting the administrative files that control users' access and allocations. For the purpose of logging in, the system treats them as ordinary users, but once they are logged in it recognises that they have special privileges. If it is felt that the ordinary security afforded to users is insufficient for the protection of these special privileges, then additional measures can be taken; it can, for example, be arranged that these privileges can only be obtained from a special console in the manager's office, and that an additional password is asked for. From time to time, system malfunctioning will inevitably occur, and the system programmers responsible for maintenance need a special way into the system for recovery and repair purposes. This is perhaps the Achilles heel of the system, and it is one of the things that was in mind when the above remarks about computer room security were written.

Management

The management of a computing centre offering time-sharing facilities presents a number of problems that were not met in the days when there was only batch processing to offer. Since the on-line users are present at their consoles when some at least of their work is being run, user scheduling has a real time aspect. Furthermore, it is no longer possible for a manager to give effect to his decisions about priority and the allocation of computer resources by issuing instructions to the operators in the computer room, since the work comes in largely along telephone lines and the operators do not handle it. A significant part of a modern operating system must, therefore, be concerned with providing the manager with the necessary tools by which he may control the flow of work in the system and the acceptance by it of new work. It is convenient to refer to the collection of packages that provide these tools by the name *management system* (Wilkes and Hartley, 1969). A management system includes routines for logging console users in and out, for checking the credentials of all users, for controlling the rate at which they use the resources allocated to them, for keeping account of resources used, and for monitoring the operation of the system.

The aim in computer centre management should be to achieve a high throughput of work while, at the same time, giving the individual users the share of the resources to which they are entitled with a minimum waste of time on their part. Above all, in times of pressure, controlling the amount of work that users can do by allowing the response to degrade should be avoided. It may not be possible to allow users to log in as often, or stay logged in for as long, as they would wish, but during the times that they are logged in they should always be given good service. Increasing the number logged in beyond a certain point will not increase the total amount of work that users can do, but will merely cause them to spend more time doing it.

From the point of view of the manager of a computing centre it makes little difference how the resources are allocated or how priorities are determined. This may be done through a price mechanism as in the case of a computing centre operating on a commercial basis, or by means of directives handed down from higher authority as, for example, in the case of a centre operating as a department within an industrial firm. This section is largely concerned with the technical means by which the manager can give effect to the decisions that he has taken, or that have been imposed upon him, and by which he can fulfil the commitments that he has entered into with his users.

It may be noted that the emphasis is on management aids and not on automated management. Management, like government, is to some extent a contest, in this case between the management and the managed. An individual user will endeavour to conduct his operations in such a way as to secure the maximum personal advantage, even if this involves adopting practices that react unfavourably on other users or lead to severe inefficiency in the operation of the system as a whole. Management will naturally take steps designed to curb anti-social behaviour and, inevitably, users will develop counter measures. For example, a system whereby files that have not been accessed for a specified period of time are archived or deleted leads to an obvious retort. Management remains an essentially human activity and the object of a management system is to enable the manager to react in a flexible manner to changing circumstances and to ensure that the centre runs in an orderly and efficient manner.

Admission to the system

A management system is concerned with, and must have means of identifying, both *users* and *projects*. One user may work on many projects and one project may have many users. Allocations of computer time and other resources may be made either to users or to projects, but it seems more logical in most circumstances that they should be made to projects. Computer resources should be allocated under various headings, separate allocations being made for the separate operating shifts. Some of the headings might be: processor time, console time, maximum core space, maximum printer output, file space on the disc, and file space in the archive system.

It is not so clear whether priority should be accorded to individual users or to individual projects, and indeed it is easy to see circumstances in which a legitimate case can be made for either arrangement. The term priority can be used in a number of different ways. However it is used, it is important to realise that priority only makes sense if the amount of work authorised for the system is within its capabilities. In an overloaded system, low priority users will get no service at all if high priority users have an unlimited allocation of time.

High priority does not necessarily go with a large allocation of time; at the highest priority level of all, one might have a user who needed only a few minutes a day for some real time experimental interaction. Although users who can claim priority should be allowed to log in at the expense of users with lower priority, unless the circumstances under which the centre operates are very unusual, it appears best to treat all users equally once they are logged in. The aim in designing a priority system should be to ensure that work on a given level of priority to which resources have been assigned should run as though there were no work of lower priority in the system. It is then possible, without prejudice to the interests of high priority users, for any surplus processor time that remains after their needs have been met to be used on work of low or zero priority, instead of being allowed to run to waste.

When a would-be on-line user presents himself, the logging-in algorithm is responsible for deciding whether his credentials are in order, whether he has system resources to his credit, and whether the state of loading of the system is such that an additional user can be accepted. If necessary, it will log out a low priority user in favour of a high priority user who wishes to come in. Preferably, a user who is forcibly logged out in this fashion should be given a few minutes in which to tidy up his affairs. If peremptory logging out without warning is necessary, then the system should save the user's status so that he can resume his work on some future occasion exactly as it was when interrupted.

On pp.43–45, the scheduling algorithm was discussed from the point of view of the system designer and its role in promoting system efficiency was emphasised. This it does by ensuring that the jobs active at any given time form a good mix from the point of view of equipment utilisation. However, since the scheduling algorithm is also responsible for selecting jobs for running from the various off-line queues, it also gives effect to management policy. The scheduling algorithm is, in fact, the place at which the responsibilities of the systems designer and the service manager meet. It is recommended that the scheduling algorithm should be so designed that on the average a constant minimum proportion of time goes to the background, the exact proportion being varied as circumstances indicate. The proportion of background run can be allowed to vary from second to second (provided that the average is maintained) in order to allow short-term peaks in foreground activity to be accommodated.

The load imposed by a user who is logged in can vary markedly according to whether he is running programs, editing files, or remaining for the time being idle. Although this variability is to some extent smoothed out when an average is taken over all the users logged in at any one time, a substantial degree of variability remains and may show a trend throughout the day. An automatic means of adjusting the number of users who are allowed to log in is, therefore, an advantage. R. Mills implemented such a system for the CTSS and gave it the name *load leveller*. The load leveller monitors the number of jobs waiting on the various queues and adjusts the number of users accordingly, forcibly logging some out or allowing new ones to log in. Since there must inevitably be a delay between a change becoming necessary and actually taking place, problems of stability familiar in control engineering arise. A discussion of automatic load adjustment from this point of view will be found in Wilkes, 1971.

A common requirement is that there should be an equitable distribution of computer usage between different sections or *divisions* of the community of users served by the system; if so, it is necessary that the logging-in program should recognise such divisions and give effect to priorities both between and within them. For example, it would not necessarily log out a low priority user who belonged to a different division from a high priority user who wanted to come in if the low priority user's division were under-subscribed. It should be noted that the need to converse with and check the credentials of users attempting to log in to a system that is full may in itself impose an appreciable load, particularly as it involves accessing the files containing users' records. It is desirable, therefore, that these records should be organised in such a way that a quick decision can be taken as to whether a user can immediately be sent away or whether further investigation of his priority rating and resource allocations would be in order. Some curtailment of the liberty of a refused user to go on making repeated attempts to log in within a short space of time may also be desirable.

When a user wished to log in to the Cambridge Multiple Access System, he was required to specify what he would require by way of system resources. If his request were within his authorisation and the loading of the system so permitted he would be logged in. Otherwise the logging-in program would make him an offer about what would be possible. For example, if he attempted to log in in the regular way—this is, in *normal mode*—and if the system were heavily loaded, he might be offered *edit mode* in which he would be able to create and edit files, but not to run jobs except in the background. If he were entitled to claim priority, and by doing so could then be admitted at the expense of someone else, then he was told so. It is always a good principle that users should have to exert any priority to which they may be entitled by an explicit act, rather than that they should be accorded it automatically. Not only does this encourage the growth of a social conscience among the users, but it also enables them to conserve their priority allocations of time for circumstances in which they really need it.

Allocations of time

If computer time is allocated to projects, then associated with each allocation must be a list of users who are entitled to draw on it. This list constitutes one of a number of *controls* that may be associated with each allocation. Other controls can specify the modes of access in which the allocation is available, and the amount of computer time and console time that may be used in a particular shift on a particular day. The last control in effect regulates the rate at which the allocation may be used and enables a particular project to be accorded a planned share of the resources available, not only over a period of time, but also on a day-to-day basis. However, users do not like to be forced off the machine when they have exhausted their allocation for a particular shift if it is obvious to them that the load is light. It is better, therefore, that they should first be declared 'vulnerable' and not forced off until their place is actually needed by another user.

Another control that may be useful is one that specifies the maximum number of users that may draw on the allocation at any one time. This enables a project to be shared, for example, by a large number of students without the students being able to monopolise the system. Again, there can be a control restricting the use of the allocation to certain consoles. This can be used for giving special facilities to consoles situated adjacent to a satellite computer or some other special piece of equipment; it can also be used for giving special facilities to consoles used by the administration. It is convenient also to be able to specify by means of a control the dates between which the allocation may be used. Apart from the obvious use of this facility, it is very convenient to be able to set up in advance a high priority allocation for the purpose of a demonstration planned for a particular day.

The above controls apply to particular allocations. It is useful in addition to have over-all controls that can be used during periods of testing, or at times when the service is not regarded as being fully available, to restrict still further what users can do. For example, the use of certain consoles only may be permitted, logging in may be restricted to administrative staff or systems programmers, or some temporary restriction may be placed on the size of job that can be created.

If priority is given to a project, then any user entitled to draw on the allocation will enjoy priority in logging in. It is not, however, normally necessary that the whole of the time allocated to a project should be of high priority. Similarly, if the management system allows priority to be accorded to an individual user personally, then it will normally be sufficient if, during each day or week, he is allowed to enjoy priority for a limited period only.

A comprehensive management system provides the manager with a wide variety of ways in which he may intervene to control the running of the system. Many of these may never be required and others only rarely. It should, however, be clearly understood that if a proper way of controlling some particular activity is not provided, then the manager may be forced to take improvised and arbitrary action that will have unfortunate side-effects.

Operational information

An important part of a management system is the routine which monitors the operations going on and provides the manager with a continuous flow of information about how the system is working and how it is being used. For example, information should be provided about the amount of filing space that users are actually using and the level of their filing activity. Users often complain that they have difficulty in logging in because the system is always full. In dealing with complaints of this kind, it is helpful if the manager has available information showing in retrospect what the average probability was, during, say, the last month, of a user being able to log in with a given priority at any particular time of day. To obtain this information, it is necessary to have a minute by minute record of the state of loading of the system and then to run a program that simulates the logging-in algorithm and computes the average probability of being able to log in as a function of time of day.

The extent and detail of the records that the manager is expected to keep for control and accounting purposes will vary from organisation to organisation. The cost involved in collecting and analysing such information is frequently not negligible; sometimes it may even be cheaper to run a short job, such as a program test, than to check whether or not the user is entitled to run it.

Role of operators

The role of machine operators in a multiple-access system is very different from their role in a batch-processing system. They are much less concerned with loading programs from punched cards, although they still have a good deal of line printer output to deal with. If the system is a large one, it is convenient to have one operator permanently stationed at the typewriter on which the supervisor prints its messages. Many of these will call for the mounting of magnetic tapes and, until the time comes when automatic tape-mounting mechanisms are available, this is likely to be a major part of the operators' work. Generally speaking, in a modern system the computer tells the operators what to do rather than the other way round. Many scheduling decisions are taken automatically and the shift leader does not bear the same responsibilities in this respect as he did in the case of older systems. The operators will have to intervene when there is a stoppage of either hardware or software. A particularly severe or unusual fault may make it necessary to restart the system from cold. The operators should be carefully trained to deal with other stoppages in a way that will minimise the disruption of the service.

File space allocation

Few installations have as much filing space on disc as they would like. This is partly because disc space is expensive and partly because continued expansion to meet increasing demand is not always technically possible, at any rate in the short term. Means must therefore be found to encourage users to delete or otherwise remove from the disc files that they have ceased to use actively. Charging a suitable rent for disc space is, of course, one way of doing this, but it is not always possible to fix the rent so that it will be a real deterrent to the keeping of unnecessary information without putting an unfair financial burden on the user who really needs a lot of disc space. It has already been remarked that automatic systems for removing from the disc files that have not been accessed for some time soon become ineffective as users develop counter-measures.

It must be recognised that users require disc space not only for long-term storage, but also for temporary working space during periods of activity. For this and a variety of other reasons it is found in practice that there are few users who make continuous use of all the disc space allocated to them. It is consequently safe to allocate a total amount of disc space substantially in excess of that physically available.

Fixed allocations of disc space give the user little incentive to prune his collection of files during periods in which he is relatively inactive. A system of allocation that avoids this disadvantage has been in use in Cambridge since the latter part of 1968, and has proved very successful. A user is given an initial *disc credit* expressed in blocks, and he is given a *daily income* also expressed in blocks. At the start of each day, the system updates his disc credit by deducting an amount equal to the number of blocks that he has in use at that moment and by adding his daily income. Thus, if the number of blocks in use is equal to the daily income, the disc credit will remain constant. Otherwise, it will either increase towards a maximum *credit bound*, B (allocated for each user), or fall towards a minimum, — B. A user who has a positive disc credit can create new files provided that his total disc usage measured in blocks does not exceed a maximum known as his *disc limit*. A user with a negative credit, on the other hand, is prevented from creating new files or updating old ones, although he can otherwise continue with his work; in order to release himself from this disability, he must delete some files or cause them to be removed from the disc and then wait until his credit becomes positive again. Note that what affects his disc credit is his overnight usage measured at the start of the day; no account is taken of his usage at other times, provided that it does not exceed his disc limit.

Daily income, disc limit, and credit bound are fixed individually for each user; commonly they are in the ratios 1:2:3 although these ratios can be varied to suit individual requirements. A user has a number of strategies open to him according to whether his requirement is primarily for long-term storage or primarily for temporary working space. If he can reduce his use of overnight disc space below his daily income, and keep it there for a period, he will build up a disc credit that will permit him to step up his overnight usage to a higher level over a limited period of time later on. A user thus has a direct incentive to delete files now in order to reap the benefit later.

References

Alderson, A., Lynch, W. C., and Randell, B. (1971). 'Thrashing in a multiprogrammed paging system.' *International Seminar on Operating System Techniques*, p. 152, Academic Press, London.

Allery, G. D. (1974). 'Data communications and public networks.' *Information Processing 74. Proc. IFIP Congress 1974*, p. 117. North-Holland, London.

Arden, B. W., Galler, B. A., O'Brien, T. C., and Westervelt, F. H. (1966). 'Program and addressing structure in a time-sharing environment.' *JACM*, Vol. 13, p. 1.

Baker, C. L. (1966). 'JOSS: introduction to a helpful assistant.' *Memorandum RM-5058-PR*, RAND Corporation.

Barron, D. W., Fraser, A. G., Hartley, D. F., Landy, B., and Needham, R. M. (1967). 'File handling at Cambridge University.' *AFIPS Conference Proc.*, Vol. 30, p. 163.

Bernstein, A. J. (1970). 'Comment on the working set model for program behaviour.' *Comm. ACM*, Vol. 13, p. 698.

Bernstein, A. J., Detlefsen, G. D., and Kerr, R. H. (1969). 'Process control and communication. *Second ACM symposium on operating system principles*, p. 60.

Bétourné, C., Boulenger, J., Ferrié, J., Kaiser, C., Krakowiak, S., and Mossière, J. (1970). 'Process management and resource sharing in the multiaccess system ESOPE.' *Comm. ACM*, Vol. 13, p. 727.

Brinch Hansen, P. (1973). 'Concurrent programming concepts.' *Comp. Surveys*, Vol. 5, p. 223.

Brinch Hansen, P. (1970). 'The nucleus of a multiprogramming system.' *Comm. ACM*, Vol. 13, p. 238.

Corbató, F. J., Merwin-Daggett, M., and Daley R. C. (1962). 'An experimental time-sharing system.' *AFIPS Conference Proc.*, Vol. 21, p. 335.

Corbató, F. J., and Vyssotsky, V. A. (1965). 'Introduction and overview of the MULTICS system.' *AFIPS Conference Proc.*, Vol. 27, p. 185.

Corbató, F. J. *et al.* (1963, 2nd ed. 1965). 'The compatible time-sharing system: a programmer guide.' M.I.T. Press, Cambridge, Mass.

Culler, G. J. (1966). 'Culler on-line system.' Univ. of California at Santa Barbara.

Culler, G. J., and Fried, B. D. (1963). 'An on-line computing center for scientific problems.' TRW Computer Div., Thompson Ramo Wooldridge Inc.

Culler, G. J., and Fried, B. D. (1965). 'The TRW two-station; on-line scientific computer; general description.' *Computer Augmentation of Human Reasoning*. Spartan Books, Washington D.C.

Daley, R. C., and Dennis, J. B. (1968). 'Virtual memory, processes, and sharing in MULTICS.' *Comm. ACM*, Vol. 11, p. 306.

Daley, R. C., and Neumann, P. G. (1965). 'A general-purpose file system for secondary storage.' *AFIPS Conference Proc.*, Vol. 27, p. 213.

Davies, D. W., Bartlett, K. A., Scantlebury, R. A., and Wilkinson, P.T. (1967). 'A digital communication network for computers giving rapid response at remote terminals.' *ACM symposium on operating system principles.*

Davis, M. R., and Ellis, T. O. (1965). 'The RAND tablet: a man-machine graphical communication device.' *AFIPS Conference Proc.*, Vol. 26, p. 325.

Dell, F. R. E. (1971). 'Features of a proposed synchronous data network.' *ACM/IEEE Second symposium on optimisation of data communication systems.*

Denning, P. J. (1968). 'Thrashing: its causes and prevention.' *AFIPS Conference Proc.*, Vol. 33, p. 915.

Denning, P. J. (1970). 'The working set model for program behaviour.' *Comm. ACM*, Vol. 13, p. 699. (See also Bernstein, A. J. (1970).)

Denning, P. J. (1970). 'Virtual memory.' *Comp. Surveys*, Vol. 2, p. 153.

Dennis, J. B. (1965). 'Segmentation and the design of multi-programmed computer systems.' *IEEE International Convention Record*, Vol. 13, Part 3, p. 214.

Dennis, J. B., and Glaser, E. L. (1965). 'The structure of on-line information processing systems.' *Information Systems Sciences: Proc. 2nd Congress*, p. 1. Spartan Books, Washington D.C.

Dennis, J. B., and Van Horn, E. C. (1966). 'Programming semantics for multiprogrammed computations.' *Comm. ACM*, Vol. 9, p. 143.

Dijkstra, E. W. (1968). 'The structure of the 'THE' multiprogramming system.' *Comm. ACM*, Vol. 11, p. 341.

England, D. M. (1972). 'Architectural features of system 250.' *Infotech State of the Art Report 14 — Operating systems*, p. 395. Infotech Information Ltd., Maidenhead.

Fabry, R. S. (1968). 'Preliminary description of a supervisor for a computer organised around capabilities.' *Quart. Prog. Report*. No. 18, Sect. IIA, Inst. Comp. Res., Univ. Chicago.

Fabry, R. S. (1971). 'List-structured addressing.' Thesis, Univ. Chicago.

Fajman, R., and Borgelt, J. (1973). 'WYLBUR: an interactive text editing and remote job entry system.' *Comm. ACM*, Vol. 16, p. 314.

Fano, R. M. (1965). 'The MAC system: the computer utility approach.' *IEEE Spectrum*, Vol. 2, p. 56

Graham, R. M. (1968). 'Protection in an information processing utility.' *Comm. ACM*, Vol. 11, p. 365.

Hartley, D. F. (1970). 'Management software in multiple-access systems.' *Bull. IMA*, Vol. 6, p. 11.

Hartley, D. F. (ed.) (1968). 'The Cambridge multiple-access system: user's reference manual.' University Mathematical Laboratory, Cambridge, England.

Hartley, D. F., Landy, B., and Needham, R. M. (1968). 'The structure of a multiprogramming supervisor.' *Computer J.*, Vol. 11, p. 247.

IBM (1966). 'System/360 Model 67. Time sharing system. Preliminary technical summary.' Form C20–1647–0.

Kilburn, T., Edwards, D. B. G., Lanigan M. J., and Sumner, F. H. (1962). 'One-level storage system.' *IRE Transactions on Electronic Computers*, Vol. EC-11, p. 223.

Kilburn, T., Howarth, D. J., Payne, R. B., and Sumner, F. H. (1961). 'The Manchester University ATLAS operating system. Part 1: internal organization.' *Computer J.*, Vol. 4, p. 222.

'The Manchester University ATLAS operating system. Part 2: users' description.' *Computer J.*, Vol. 4, p. 226.

REFERENCES

Kurtz, T. E., and Lochner, K. M. (1965). 'Supervisory systems for the Dartmouth time-sharing system.' *Computers and Automation*, Vol. 14, No. 10, p. 25.

Lampson, B. W. (1968). 'A scheduling philosophy for multiprocessing systems.' *Comm. ACM*, Vol. 11, p. 347.

Loopstra, B. J. (1959). 'Input and output in the X-1 system.' *Proc. UNESCO Conf. on Information Processing*, p. 342. Butterworths, London.

McCarthy, J., Boilen, S., Fredkin, E., and Licklider, J. C. R. (1963). 'A time-sharing debugging system for a small computer.' *AFIPS Conference Proc.*, Vol. 23, p. 51.

Needham, R. M. (1970). 'Software engineering techniques and operating system design and production. '*Software Engineering Techniques*, N.A.T.O. Science Council, Brussels, p. 111.

Needham, R. M. (1972). 'Protection systems and protection implementations.' *AFIPS Conference Proc.*, Vol. 41, Part 1, p 571.

Needham, R. M., and Hartley, D. F. (1969). 'Theory and practice in operating system design.' *Second ACM symposium on operating system principles*, p.8.

Needham, R. M., and Wilkes, M. V. (1974). 'Domains of protection and the management of processes.' *Computer J.*, Vol. 17, p. 117.

Organick, E. I. (1972). 'The MULTICS system: an examination of its structure.' M.I.T. Press, Cambridge, Mass.

Purdy, G. E. (1974) 'A high security log-in procedure.' *Comm. ACM*, Vol. 17, p. 442.

Roberts, L. G., and Wessler, B. D. (1970). 'Computer network developments to achieve resource sharing.' *AFIPS Conference Proc.*, Vol. 36, p. 543.

Schroeder, M. D. (1971), 'Performance of the GE-645 associative memory while MULTICS is in operation.' *ACM SIGOPS workshop on system performance evaluation*, p. 227.

Schroeder, M. D., and Saltzer, J. H. (1972). 'A hardware architecture for implementing protection rings.' *Comm. ACM*. Vol. 15, p. 157.

Schwartz, J. I., Coffman, E. G., and Weissman, C. (1964). 'A general-purpose time-sharing system.' *AFIPS Conference Proc.* Vol. 25, p. 397.

Shaw, J. C. (1964). 'JOSS: a designer's view of an experimental on-line computing system.' *AFIPS Conference Proc.* Vol. 26, p. 455.

Spier, M. J., and Organick, E. I. (1969). 'The MULTICS interprocess communication facility.' *Second ACM symposium on operating system principles*, p. 83.

Tymes, L. (1971). 'TYMNET—a terminal oriented communication network.' *AFIPS Conference Proc.*, Vol. 38, p. 211.

Van Horn, E. C. (1966). 'Computer design for asynchronously reproducible multiprocessing.' NAC-TR-34, M.I.T., Cambridge, Mass.

Vyssotsky, V. A., Corbató, F. J., and Graham, R. M. (1965). 'Structure of the MULTICS supervisor.' *AFIPS Conference Proc.*, Vol. 27, p. 203.

Whitfield, H., and Wight, A. S. (1973). 'EMAS — The Edinburgh multi-access system.' *Computer J.*, Vol. 16, p. 331.

Wilkes, M. V. (1965). 'Slave memories and dynamic storage allocation.' *IEEE Transactions on Electronic Computers*, Vol. EC-14, p. 270.

Wilkes, M. V. (1969). 'A model for core space allocation in a time-sharing system.' *AFIPS Conference Proc*, Vol. 34, p. 265.

Wilkes, M. V., and Hartley, D. F. (1969). 'The management system; a new species of software?' *Datamation*, Vol. 15, No. 9 (September), p. 73.

Wilkes, M. V. (1971). 'Automatic load adjustment in time-sharing systems.' *ACM SIGOPS workshop on system performance evaluation*, p. 308.

Wilkes, M. V. (1972). 'On preserving the integrity of data bases.' *Computer J.*, Vol. 15, p. 191.

Wilkes, M. V. (1973). 'The Cambridge Multiple-access system in retrospect.' *Software Pract. Exper.*, Vol. 3, p. 323.

Wilkes, M. V. (1973). 'The dynamics of paging.' *Computer J.*, Vol. 16, p. 1.

Index

Names of authors are in *italics*

164

165

166